Growth Counseling for Marriage Enrichment

Creative Pastoral Care and Counseling Series
Editor: Howard J. Clinebell, Jr.
Associate Editor: Howard W. Stone

Growth Counseling for Marriage Enrichment

Pre-Marriage and the Early Years

Howard J. Clinebell, Jr.

Fortress Press Philadelphia

"Freud supplied to us the sick half of psychology and we must now fill it out with the healthy half. Perhaps this health psychology will give us more possibility for controlling and improving our lives and for making ourselves better people. Perhaps this will be more fruitful than asking 'how to get *unsick.'* "*

—Abraham Maslow

Biblical quotations from the Revised Standard Version of the Bible, copyrighted 1946 and 1952 by the Division of Christian Education of the National Council of the Churches of Christ in the United States of America, are used by permission.

Library of Congress Catalog Card Number 74–26335

ISBN 0–8006–0551–9

Fourth Printing 1982

9844F82   Printed in the United States of America   1-551

Contents

Series Foreword

Let me share with you some of the hopes that are in the minds of those of us who helped to develop this series—hopes that relate directly to you as the reader. It is our desire and expectation that these books will be of help to you in developing better working tools as a minister-counselor. We hope that they will do this by encouraging your own creativity in developing more effective methods and programs for helping people live life more fully. It is our intention in this series to affirm the many things you have going for you as a minister in helping troubled persons—the many assets and resources from your religious heritage, your role as the leader of a congregation, and your unique relationship to individuals and families throughout the life cycle. We hope to help you reaffirm the *power of the pastoral* by the use of fresh models and methods in your ministry.

The aim of the series is not to be comprehensive with respect to topics but rather to bring innovative approaches to some major types of counseling. Although the books are practice-oriented, they also provide a solid foundation of theological and psychological insights. They are written primarily for ministers (and those preparing for the ministry), but we hope that they will also prove useful to other counselors who are interested in the crucial role of spiritual and value issues in all helping relationships. In addition we hope that the series will be useful in seminary courses, clergy support groups, continuing education workshops, and lay befriender training.

This is a period of rich new developments in counseling and psychotherapy. The time is ripe for a flowering of creative methods and insights in pastoral care and counseling. Our expectation is that this series will stimulate grass roots creativity as innovative methods and programs come alive for you.

Some of the major thrusts that will be discussed in this series include a new awareness of the unique contributions of the theologically trained counselor, the liberating power of the human potentials orientation, an appreciation of the pastoral-care function of the ministering congregation, the importance of humanizing systems and institutions as well as close relationships, the importance of pastoral *care* (and not just counseling), the many opportunities for caring ministries throughout the life cycle, the deep changes in male-female relationships, and the new psychotherapies—for example, Gestalt therapy, transactional analysis, educative counseling, and crisis methods. Our hope is that this series will enhance your resources for your ministry to persons, by opening doorways to understanding of these creative thrusts in pastoral care and counseling.

Howard J. Clinebell, Jr., the author of this volume, here demonstrates many of these major thrusts of the series in what I believe to be the best of his many excellent books. I see the volume as the natural outgrowth of his work for seventeen years as Professor of Pastoral Counseling at the School of Theology at Claremont—and indeed of his entire ministry including his years in the parish. His emphasis in pastoring, teaching, and writing has always been on prevention and growth as opposed to pathology and remediation. This present book brings that emphasis to its sharpest focus as it reflects his many years of experience and the experiences which he and his wife Charlotte have recently enjoyed together professionally in co-leading marriage enrichment groups.

When I first saw the manuscript I began to experiment with the "Intentional Marriage Method" and several other of the fully detailed techniques. It was through actively trying what Howard Clinebell suggests that I recognized the usefulness of what he proposes. And I urge you, the reader, to do the same: try, experiment, test, find what works best for you. The author's approach is geared to helping couples in our turbulent time. His excitement about new ways of doing this is contagious.

HOWARD W. STONE

Is This Book for You?

This book should be useful to you if you are a minister or marriage counselor who wants to increase your skills in using growth-oriented counseling and enrichment methods, or if you are an individual or couple who wants to learn some practical methods by which to help people (yourself and others) develop more intimate, liberating, and mutually fulfilling marriages. Chapters 6 and 7 focus on the needs of couples before marriage and during the early years. However, the basic methods described throughout the book can be used at any stage of marriage.

You should know that I hope to do four things in these pages: (1) describe a human-potentials approach to counseling and enrichment called "growth counseling," (2) show how you can use this approach to enrich ordinary marriages, (3) apply the approach to helping couples use marriage crises as growth opportunities, (4) present various working models for ministers and lay leaders to use in developing enrichment workshops and counseling programs for their church. These approaches also can be used in schools and social agencies.

In recent years, I've heard pastors ask questions like the ones I also asked during my decade in the parish ministry—

1) How can we develop an effective program to prevent marriage disasters?

2) How can we encourage couples to get the counseling they need sooner—before they're "coming apart at the seams"?

3) Is there a way to improve my "premarital counseling"?

4) How can our church give better support to young couples during the rough first five years of marriage?

5) How can we help couples discover there's much more to marriage than they've found so far?

6) How can healthy married couples provide a community of caring and mutual support for marriages?

7) How can we help couples who want to live their religion but haven't a clue for going about it?

8) How can our church relate constructively to couples experimenting with radical new life-styles and "hang loose" sex practices?

On a personal level, along with many other ministers and their spouses, I'm forced to ask even more pressing questions about myself and my marriage partner:

1) In the pressure-cooker of my job, what can we do to nurture our own growth?

2) Where can we enrich our own marriage?

3) How can we cope with our painful crises constructively?

4) I'm supposed to be an enlivener of other people's marriages, but how do I keep the enlivener alive?

This book won't answer all these questions—at least not fully and certainly not in ways that can be applied ready-made in your unique situation. But I will suggest approaches that have helped me both personally and professionally.

I'm excited about the methods and models of ministry of which I shall speak. I have found that they work, at least for me. And I hope your enthusiasm will increase as you discover that growth counseling opens up a fresh and better chapter in your work with people.

This book presents a model of mutual ministry and a model of the church or temple—whenever I say "church" I also mean "temple"—as a human fulfillment and training center. It offers a variety of methods to implement these models in a creative ministry to marriages. I'm pleased to be able to share with you these approaches which have emerged from my experiences.

I want to express my appreciation to Mary Anne Parrott and Catherine Jones who did the typing, to Linda Terrill and Hendrik Venter who helped prepare the manuscript, to Charlotte H. Clinebell who read it and gave me helpful feedback, and to the scores of persons from whom I have learned through the years.

HOWARD J. CLINEBELL, JR.

1. Growth Counseling— A Human Potentials Approach

> The future lies with those who believe salvation likelier to spring from the imagination of possibility than from the delineation of the historical. . . . Perhaps we all need to be reminded of the necessity of remaining open to new, or newly recovered ways of being.* —Carolyn G. Heilbrun

> Every age but ours has had its model, its ideal. All of these have been given up by our culture. . . . Perhaps we shall soon be able to use as our guide and model the fully growing and self-fulfilling human being, the one in whom all . . . potentialities are coming to full development.† —Abraham Maslow

Gradually, over the last ten years or so, my counseling and caring ministry has shifted from a diagnostic, treatment approach (a pathology model) to a human development, positive-potentials approach (a growth model). I've changed from focusing on what's wrong with a person or relationship and now I place greater emphasis on what's right and what's possible; as this change has taken place better results have occurred in my ministry of counseling, teaching, and working with small groups. Furthermore, it has gradually become clear to me that the positive approach frees one in helping relationships to use more of the rich assets and resources which every church-related, religiously aware person has available. When I've discussed growth approaches in workshops for ministers and lay persons, most participants have responded with interest, many with enthusiasm. The same has happened in workshops for counselors from various secular professions. Many ministers and counselors seem ready, even eager, to diminish their emphasis on a repair-and-rescue approach and increase their

*For this and all other notes in this book, see the Notes section beginning on p. 81.

1

emphasis on prevention through releasing the positive potentials of persons.

The Dual Nature of Growth Counseling

Growth counseling is a way of helping people to discover in themselves and in others what Buber called "the treasure of eternal possibility and the task of unearthing it."* It involves two inter-related things—a perspective on people and a set of methods.

First, there is the growth perspective, a liberating way of viewing persons (including yourself) in terms of (1) their present strengths and their rich unused capacities—intellectually, spiritually, interpersonally, creatively; (2) their profound inner strivings to fulfill more of these good gifts of life; (3) the pull of a better future toward which they can move by the fuller use of their inner riches. Viewing people through this growth perspective is one of the most important things we can do to help them grow!

Second, growth counseling involves a variety of growth-stimulating methods to help people use more of their potentialities by (1) developing better communication with self, others, nature, and God—the four basic relationships within which all growth occurs; (2) developing new skills of relating in mutually-affirming, mutually-fulfilling ways; (3) growing by making constructive decisions and taking responsible *action;* (4) using the growth possibilities inherent in each life stage; (5) learning to use the pain and problems of unexpected crises as growth opportunities; (6) learning better methods of spiritual growth—the maturing of one's personal faith, working values, sense of purpose, peak experiences, and awareness of really *belonging* in the universe.

Growth marriage counseling is only one of many applications of this general approach to liberating the potential of people. But church-related counselors probably have more opportunities as growth enablers in marriage and family relationships than in any other area.

Hope-Centered Counseling

Growth counseling is hope-oriented counseling. Hope exerts a powerful pull toward constructive change. Conversely, hopelessness is a powerful block to such change. Therefore, these methods aim explicitly at mobilizing realistic hope in the lives of individuals or couples. I suspect that hope is the most neglected force for helping human beings change. Growth methods don't ignore pain, conflict, and problems—the messy, grubby side of any marriage. To do so would paralyze growth by denying reality. This has been the weakness of the "positive thinking" approaches. Growth counseling methods help people deal with their pain in the context of reality-based hope. This not only makes the pain look very different but also releases remarkable energies for coping constructively with the pain!

Growth marriage counseling is a way of helping people cope constructively with problems and conflicts. It uses many of the methods of traditional couple marriage counseling, but it adds a vigorous, sustained emphasis on hope-creating awareness of the couple's past successes—however limited—their present strengths, and their ability to create a better future by using more of their assets.

Faith (in the sense of trust), hope, and love are, as the First Letter to the Corinthians says so beautifully, crucial and lasting dynamics in all good human relationships, especially intimate ones like marriage. But when things are going badly and all three have grown faint, hope is the power by which trust and love are revitalized, and with these three a marriage is reborn.

The same is true in monotonous marriages in which couples are resigned to flat, two-dimensional relationships. Only if the power of hope is released will they discover the latent marriage that is theirs, a marriage with more heights and depths, more aliveness and conflict, more zest, pain, and fulfillment than they had imagined. The growth approach aims at helping a couple actualize hope by learning new skills for nourishing rather than starving their love!

A Third-Force Approach

The "third force" in psychology and psychotherapy—the human potentials, value-oriented approaches—provides much of the theoretical foundation for growth counseling. (The first and second forces are psychoanalysis and behaviorism.) The towering figure in the third force, the late Abraham Maslow, distinguished between deficiency needs and growth needs. Traditional psychotherapy, he pointed out, concentrated mainly on persons suffering massive deficiences of their basic psychological needs for security, love, and esteem. In studies of "self-actualizing" people he found that a new need emerges in persons who have learned to satisfy their basic needs. Their new need is to continue to grow by developing their creativity and their unused potentialities.

I find that an awareness of the persistent but often hidden growth strivings in people is immensely useful in counseling with those suffering from major basic need hungers—for example, couples with deeply pained lives and troubled marriages. This awareness is indispensable in enriching normal marriages.

The distinction between deficiency and growth needs provides a guideline for keeping balance in one's helping activities. The distinction points to the two sides of the counseling and pastoral care coin—counseling/healing and nurture/prevention. As every parish minister knows, marriage counseling is both unavoidable and a vital form of human help. But the church is also called to be a growth-nurture-training center for the vast majority of a congregation who do not need "counseling" at any given time. Unfortunately, in recent decades, counseling has tended to be the tail that wagged the pastoral care dog. It is more productive to make the nurturing of "normal" people throughout the life cycle normative. For me, this means investing at least three times as much caring time and leadership (ministerial and lay) in person-building, human enrichment activities (including short-term growth-oriented counseling) as in helping those with deep deficiency needs through longer-term pastoral counseling.

The growth counselor can use the human potentials and lifelong development perspectives as the hub of the wheel around which insights and methods from the newer growth-oriented psychotherapies—e.g., reality therapy, transactional analysis, gestalt therapy, action therapies—can be integrated. The growth perspective also allows the integration into one's approach of growth-enhancing insights from the older psyco-therapies—Jungian, Adlerian, Rankian, and Freudian.

Growth counseling blends third-force thinking with what I call the "fourth force" in psychology and counseling—relationship-building methods including couple marriage counseling, conjoint family therapy, couple group counseling, and multiple-family support groups. In contrast to intra-psychic and one-to one methods, these approaches seek to liberate directly an entire relationship system—a marriage, family, or group—so that everyone in that network will be freer to grow. These methods take seriously the fact that, for better or worse, we are inescapably "members one of another" (Eph. 4:25). Growth or stagnation results from the quality of our relationship!

Liberating the Power of the Pastoral

Growth counseling can help one strengthen an authentic theological and pastoral identity in caring and counseling work. And when I use the term "pastoral" I clearly do not mean to exclude, but precisely to include, the ministry of the laity. Growth counseling can help us church-related counselors use more of our seven unique resources:

Biblical Insights

Growth counseling enables us to rediscover and implement growth-centered, people-liberating insights that are deep in our biblical heritage. These insights, which have been restated beautifully in the relational and growth-oriented philosophy of Martin Buber, are energizers. When they touch the heart of an individual or a group or a church, they stimulate the flow of new creative energies. Human potentials thinkers such as Maslow affirm in modern psychological language deep, neglected dimensions in our spiritual heritage. Let's look at some growth-oriented biblical insights.

The ancient insights that we human beings are children of God (Rom. 8:16) and that our spirits are formed in the divine image (Gen. 1:27) express the awareness that each of us has tremendous possibilities within us. The fulfillment of these possibilities is awaited "with eager longing" by the whole creation (Rom. 8:19). Think of it! All of life is on the side of growth and fulfillment.

The growth parables—the leaven (Matt. 13:33; Luke 13:21), the mustard seed (Matt. 13:31; Mark 4:31; Luke 13:19), the sower (Matt. 13:3; Mark 4:3; Luke 8:5), the talents (Matt. 25:14-15)—all have new meaning for me since I've been turned on by the growth perspective. They refer to the way God's kingdom—the new kind of world of love and justice—is coming, by growing! And we all are invited to participate in this growth process.

Jesus' basic life-style was people-creating. This is seen most clearly in his remarkable skill of drawing forth extraordinary gifts from "ordinary people." He could "see" in a fisherman with obvious weaknesses an underlying potential for rocklike strength. And so he called Simon by a new name—Peter, which means "rock." By looking at people in terms of their becoming, Jesus helped enable them to become! That was "good news"—a new quality of relationships is possible and in these relationships a new quality of human consciousness can develop. That *was* good news in the first century; it *is* good news today—news that is needed in our inner lives, our marriages, our churches, and our world. In the Fourth Gospel, Jesus' purpose in coming is described as enabling people to find life "in all its fullness" (John 10:10 NEB). Life in all its fullness—this is what growth counseling is about. What a beautiful theme for a growth-centered church and ministry!

Time-tested biblical insights about the resistance to growth provide a healthy corrective to the unrealistic optimism which sometimes appears in the human potentials movement. What's wrong with simple nature analogies—for example, "We're all seeds becoming plants, becoming flowers"? The growth forces *are* in us, as in a seed. But there are also complex, persistent forces in human beings and in society which resist growth. The biblical awareness is that we often use our freedom to cut ourselves off from those very growth-empowering relationships for which our hearts long. This points to a reality which can't be ignored if we're going to be growth enablers. Whether called by the traditional religious word "sin" or by the traditional psychotherapeutic word "resistance," it must be dealt with. The biblical awareness is that a dying must precede every rebirth—that our personal Easters cannot occur unless that which keeps us from experiencing the resurrection of awareness and caring dies. Thus, growth is often painful and anxiety-arousing as well as joyful and energizing. It hurts to let go of something, however constricting, that has at least made us feel protected. Growth involves risking. It requires the "leap of trust."

The biblical insights about resources for growth are also important. Like life itself, all growth is a gift and a mystery. Growth occurs through a process which releases energies from beyond ourselves as well as within ourselves. We can choose whether we will participate in this enlivening process or not, but we need not and cannot create the growth energies. The awareness that all growth is a gift of God, the creative Spirit, helps get us out of the center. The challenge we all face is to learn to facilitate the flow of the growth-enabling energies of the universe *through* our relationships.

A Fellowship of Persons-in-Relationship

Growth counseling enables us to use more fully the rich opportunities which are inherent in the fact (which we usually take for granted) that a church is a fellowship, a network of groups, individuals, and families. Relationships are both the place and the power of growth. Church-related counselors have direct, regular entree to a wide variety of relationships. Growth counseling can help persons "turn on to life through people." Having an ongoing relationship with a majority or near-majority of families in most communities creates a unique opportunity for churches that is shared by no other social institution. Growth groups, combining mutual nurturing and relationship training, provide better tools than ever before to utilize this opportunity. In responding to this opportunity, churches are discovering deeper meanings in the New Testament image of the church as the body of Christ (1 Cor. 10:16; Eph. 4:12).

Personal Contacts Throughout the Life Cycle

Growth counseling enables us to help each other use the developmental crisis of each life stage as a growth opportunity. As the only institutions with ongoing face-to-face contact with "normal" people throughout the life cycle, churches have a unique opportunity to help people use the extended life-span given us by medical progress. To do this effectively, a church should become a lifelong learning and growth center.

Natural Contacts With Persons in Crises

The growth-counseling approach also enhances a counselor's ability to use his/her natural contacts with many persons going through unexpected crises such as sickness, bereavement, and divorce. Short-term, action-oriented crisis-counseling methods (one aspect of growth counseling) are a "natural" for a minister or lay befriender. Such methods often are effective in a few sessions, allowing persons in crises to rally inner strengths and learn better ways of coping.

Christian Life-Style as Responsible Action

Growth counseling, being decision-oriented and action-centered, draws on another strength in our tradition—the fact that the Christian life-style is a way of living, not just a way of believing. Personal growth often occurs more quickly by helping a person make a decision and take responsible action than by focusing mainly on changing feelings and attitudes.

Ordinary People in Mutual Ministry

The growth approach helps to mobilize the power of ordinary people to help each other through mutual ministry. The individuals in every congregation who have the capacity for this ministry of growth are a gold mine of largely untapped helping resources. Their abilities can be released through a systematic training-for-caring program.

The Focus on Spiritual Development

Growth counseling, by recognizing that spiritual development is at the center of all truly human growth, allows us to use the unique resources of our religious heritage and theological training in our counseling and enrichment work. Today, with the collapse of the old "certainties," many people suffer from value-confusion, meaning-emptiness, childish consciences, and theological future shock. The ability to be a spiritual-growth enabler has never been more important.

Pastoral growth counseling moves beyond the third and fourth forces in counseling and therapy to the "fifth force"— by which I mean insights and methods of spiritual counseling and growth. Recognizing that "the spiritual" is what is uniquely human, growth counseling brings the resources of one's religious heritage to the task of facilitating the maturing of one's faith, conscience, and relationship with God. The goal is a liberated and liberating spirit, open to experiencing the truth that makes us free (John 8:32)—free to grow, free to love and care, free to make a constructive impact on society, free to become all that the Creator dreamed for us to become!

2. The Intentional Marriage Method— A Basic Growth Tool

Genuine responsibility exists only where there is real responding . . . to what is to be seen and heard and felt.*

—Martin Buber

One important aspect of a good love relationship, is what may
be called need identification, or the pooling of the hierarchies
of basic needs in two persons into a single hierarchy. The
effect of this is that one person feels another's needs as if they
were his own and for that matter also feels his own needs to
some extent as if they belonged to the other.†

—Abraham Maslow

How can we help couples—ourselves and others—learn to
develop more liberating, mutually-fulfilling relationships? How
can we apply the growth-counseling approach to marriage?
Before discussing this on a level of theory, I'd like to invite
you to *experience* the growth approach. Whether you're a
pastor, a counselor, or a lay person, the best way to learn to
use growth methods is to try them yourself.

At the close of a marriage enrichment workshop (co-led
by Charlotte and myself) one woman wrote in her evaluation:
"The *most* helpful thing was to tell your spouse the things you
like and appreciate in him . . . also to tell him your needs. We
haven't done that in twenty-three years of marriage!" The
experience to which she referred is the heart of our approach
to both marriage enrichment and growth-centered marriage
counseling. Over the last five years, a majority of those who
have participated in our marriage workshops and groups have
identified this as the "most helpful" part of the experience and
the "most useful" tool they acquired. It's called the "Inten-

tional Marriage Method," which we can call IMM for short. It's a simple, four-step tool that a couple can use on their own to help their marriage grow in the directions they desire.

The IMM sounds so simple, it's hard to believe it could work so well. But I hope you'll try it. If you're married, invite your spouse to join you in experiencing the IMM. If you're single, invite a close friend (of either sex) to join you in learning the method. Enjoy yourselves while you learn!

The Growth Formula

Personal growth occurs whenever human beings experience two things in the same relationship—an affirming love that we don't have to earn, and honest openness. This is the "growth formula": CARING + CONFRONTATION = GROWTH! The truth stated theologically is, of course, the same: grace (the love one doesn't have to earn, because it's there in the relationship) + judgment (confrontation with how one is hurting or limiting the growth of oneself or others) = movement toward greater wholeness. The growth formula helps one understand why healing and creative change occur in some counseling, education, enrichment groups, marriages, and preaching, yet not in others.

Both parts of the formula are essential. In traditional Christian terms both law and gospel are necessary. Acceptance without honest confrontation is experienced as incomplete acceptance. Confrontation without caring and acceptance is experienced as judgmentalism and rejection. A relationship stimulates growth when persons can "speak the truth in love" (Eph. 4:15 NEB), as the New Testament describes the growth formula.

Growth counseling aims at implementing this formula in helping relationships. The IMM uses the formula to let you build on whatever you have going for you in your marriage (or other close relationship). It can be useful to many couples —from those with chronic conflicts to those with "happy" marriages which include a mixture of pain and joy. The IMM allows couples to reduce their pain and increase their mutual satisfaction.

The IMM in Four Steps
Identifying and Affirming the Strengths of Your Relationship

We usually introduce the IMM in a group or retreat by saying to the couples:

Let's become aware of more of the positive strengths in our marriages as a basis for meeting more of our needs. Each couple please find a comfortable place to sit facing each other somewhere in the room, not too close to other couples. Sit on the floor if you like./ (I'll use this slash to mean that the task just described is now to be completed.)

OK. Begin the Intentional Marriage Method by one of you completing the sentence, "I appreciate in you . . . " as many times as you can. Tell the person all the things you really like. For example, I may say to my co-leader, "Honey, I appreciate your hair" (or) "I appreciate the ways you enjoy using your mind." The other person just listens, receiving these affirmations. As soon as one person finishes, the other does the same thing, completing the sentence, "I appreciate in you . . ."/

(In leading groups or retreats Charlotte and I usually take part in the structured couple experiences. We don't want to appear in the manipulative position of asking others to do what we seem unwilling to do ourselves. Besides, we find that it actually helps our marriage.)

Now discuss how you feel about what you have just done./

Write on a card all the things you can remember that your partner appreciated in you./

Your communication skills can be improved by practice, so look at each other's lists and see how well you listened to each other./

I hope this first step helped you get in touch with many of the strengths and assets in your marriage; these provide a foundation on which to build in the steps that follow.

Identifying Growth Areas—Unmet Needs/Wants in Each Person

One way to improve your marriage is to state your needs and wants clearly and directly. In this second step complete the sentence, "I need from you . . ." Begin as in step one with one person and then give the other equal opportunity to list his or her needs. For instance, I may say to my partner, "I need more time alone with you, time when just you and I can be together" (or) "I need for you to touch me more." It's important for each of you to get your separate list of needs out on the table before you discuss them./

Now discuss how you feel about this part of the experience./

List on the reverse side of your own card all the needs expressed by your partner./

Now check each other's lists and discuss how well you heard each other this time./

This next part may seem a bit tedious but it's important. Working together, pick out those needs which are the same or similar on both lists and put an A beside them./

Now put a C beside the needs on your two lists that conflict or collide—for example, one of you needs or wants more frequent sex and the other less./

Now put a B beside the needs that are left, those that don't contradict the other's but are simply different./

Recontracting for Change—Deciding to Meet More of Your Needs

Now you're ready to make things more mutually satisfying for yourselves. Discuss the A needs on your lists and decide on one shared need which seems both important and achievable to you both. It's important to experience success as you begin to improve things. After you have picked an A need as your marriage-growth goal, plan exactly how and when you'll take action to meet it.

To practice the skill of making a clear, workable change plan, write out a brief, joint description of the need and of your plan to meet it. Describe the changes you intend to make in terms of each person's behavior, that is, what you each plan to *do*. This written description will allow you to check back later and know when you've done it./

Congratulations! You have just used the skill of writing a small but significant new clause in your marriage agreement or covenant!

Taking Action—Checking Out the Plan, Implementing It, and
Keeping Track of Progress

The final step in the IMM is to meet your shared need by implementing your plan. It helps in doing this to use a growth-support couple or a small group of couples committed to encouraging each other's growth. So find another couple with whom to share your plan (or, in a retreat you might suggest: join with three other couples with whom you'd like to get better acquainted)./

Now share your plans, giving each other feedback. Give each other encouragement and raise questions about anything that may need clarifying or strengthening to make the plans more workable./

Discuss your experience in checking out your plans, including how you might continue to use a sharing group for mutual support and growth./

In taking action to make your marriage more mutually fulfilling it helps to keep a record of your ongoing progress (or regress) in working out your plans. For instance, if you decided you both need a regular time each day to communicate, keep tab on yourself so you'll know how you're doing and can plan your next step accordingly. Some couples do this in a Marriage Growth Diary; in it they also make daily entries of their significant events, sharings, and insights.

How to Move Ahead

After you've had your first success using the IMM, and feel the rewards of satisfying a mutual need, move on to another shared need and devise a plan to meet it. Repeat the "I appreciate . . ." step regularly in order to keep in touch with your positive feelings and strengths.

If you tried the IMM and it didn't work, remember, it takes practice to master any new skill. In the complexities of being human and married, one can't "win 'em all." Don't waste valuable energy blaming each other or analyzing why you "blew it." Instead, use your energy to create a more workable change plan, or simply choose another need. Are you both committed to meeting the need you selected? If one of you is giving in to please the other, forget about that goal for now and pick one about which you're both enthusiastic. Use your support group to strengthen your plan and affirm your efforts, however minimal your initial success.

Satisfying More Difficult Needs

After you've learned to use the IMM to satisfy several *shared* needs—the easiest place to make a difference in your marriage—move on to type B needs which don't contradict each other but also don't coincide. To use the IMM here a new skill is required: You must learn to negotiate a mutual agreement which satisfies one need of each person.

Learning to satisfy type C needs—those that are in conflict —is the most difficult. It requires two skills: negotiation and compromise to find the fair midpoint where both feel partially satisfied. (See the discussion of conflict resolution below, pp. 35-36.)

Some couples build up growth momentum by successfully meeting a series of shared and nonconflicting needs. This momentum makes it easier to negotiate a creative compromise of conflicting needs. When persons are feeling hungry emotionally, perhaps unloved or unappreciated, it's almost impossible to resolve conflicting needs. Also, accepting what one can't change in the area of conflicting needs in a marriage is easier if the satisfaction quotient is already rising.

The IMM: Recontracting

Some couples work out personal covenants or contracts— often in writing so that there'll be no misunderstanding—before the wedding or at regular intervals during a marriage. Items covered often include: (1) division of household chores; (2) the agreement concerning having, adopting, or not having children; (3) responsibility for child rearing; (4) career plans for both spouses; (5) obligations in various areas such as work, leisure, religion, community, and social life; (6) range of permissible relations beyond the marriage; (7) property, legal, and inheritance rights; (8) grounds for splitting; (9) frequency of renegotiating the agreement.

The IMM is a workable model for renegotiating the marriage covenant or agreement. It can be used to work out such an understanding for the first time or to modify ineffective parts of a previously implicit covenant. The objection that recontracting is "too legalistic" is valid only if a couple has already achieved the kind of mutually acceptable level of fairness in the marriage that lets their love flower fully. Love flows from justice and mutual fulfillment in a marriage. Furthermore, our needs change at each stage in marriage; it's essential to update our working understanding regularly in order to satisfy emerging needs.

Broadening Your Growth Goals

The process begun in using the IMM should not stop with simple quid pro quo agreements—I'll meet your needs if you'll meet mine. As love and trust grow, each person's needs increasingly include the satisfying of the partner's needs. When this occurs, any apparent conflict between *self*-actualization and *marriage*-actualization (or enrichment) gives way to the awareness that *self-other* actualization is, in the long run, the only real self-actualization. As Buber makes clear, true actualization is living in a new creative unity in which both persons are enhanced and fulfilled in their uniqueness. Self-transcendence is essential for self-fulfillment. Self-transcendence doesn't mean self-negation. It means becoming a more fulfilled self through sharing in a fulfilling relationship.

If a couple's growth goals are entirely self-centered or marriage-centered, it is important to offer them an opportunity to broaden their goals. What they *want* may not coincide with what they *need* to develop their full marriage potential. After a couple has learned to use the IMM, to satisfy their mutual heart hungers (deficiency needs), their understanding of what they need in order to continue to grow may be broadened in these ways: (1) Discussion in counseling, or in a group, of the various ways in which one's own marriage growth is enhanced by becoming a positive influence in the growth of others. (2) Confrontation by the example of other couples who have discovered the pay-off in their marriage which results from a "cause" that turns them on. (3) Values clarification exercises to confront the inadequacy of in-turning values. (4) A gentle but firm confrontation, by the leader or by group members, with the pay-off of enlarging their marital horizons by making their circles of concern more inclusive.

The Christian Life-Style and the IMM

The IMM (and the growth formula which it implements) expresses central, interdependent emphases in Jewish and Christian theology—and in other religious and humanist traditions, of course—the emphases on love, freedom, responsibility, and justice. It assumes that we have the power and the freedom to help create our own marriage futures by changing our relationship intentionally rather than drifting.

The Christian life-style *is* intentional but it is more. The *direction* of growth is crucial. The Christian understanding challenges us to self-investment in the needs of the world. We can't have dead-end marriages without becoming stagnant. Individual families can remain healthy, creative, and enriched only if they are involved in enriching others in the wider human family. To paraphrase a familiar New Testament insight: The marriage which tries to hoard (or save) its life will, in the end, lose its real vitality. Only by investing your marriage in the needs of humankind can you find the greatest depths of enrichment for yourselves.

3. Making Good Marriages Better

There is genuine dialogue—no matter whether spoken or silent—where each of the participants really has in mind the other or others in their present and particular being and turns to them with the intention of establishing a living mutual relation.*   —Martin Buber

Loving perception, whether as between sweethearts or as between parents and children, produced kinds of knowledge that were not available to nonlovers.†   —Abraham Maslow

In most marriages there's a hidden marriage waiting to be discovered and liberated. This latent marriage is a better marriage—more fulfilling, more intimate, more alive—than the here-and-now relationship. The latent marriage may be well hidden—buried under many layers of anger, mutual neglect, and hurting. Many couples aren't aware of their latent marriage. They're unaware that they're using only a small part— 15 to 25 percent perhaps—of their capacities for satisfying communication, sexual pleasure, and mutually fulfilling love. It's the unlived life in our marriages that makes them so vulnerable in crises we otherwise could take in stride.

The growth perspective sees marriage as a changing, developing process—a co-creation which the two partners continue to enrich (or gradually starve) by the ways they communicate and care for each other. A couple has the power to develop their latent marriage by nurturing each other's heart hungers—the hungers for affirming communication, warm caring, mutual esteem and trust, closeness and companionship, sexual and other enjoyment.

If couples have been deeply alienated or strangling each other's creativity for years, their latent marriage can probably be developed—if at all—only by a process of marriage therapy or long-term marriage counseling. But for the vast majority of us whose marriages are a mixture of pain and joy, frustration and satisfaction, distance and closeness—for us enrichment methods and short-term crisis methods can be effective in improving our relationships by developing our hidden marriage assets. To help couples learn to do this is one of the rich opportunities of any minister, counselor, or lay befriender.

The Crisis in Marriage

The institution of marriage is being challenged today in unprecedented ways. For every three couples that marry, one couple gets a divorce. Many youth and young adults are rejecting the validity or necessity of marriage in its traditional forms. The widespread changes in attitudes and practices, taken together, constitute a profound and accelerating social "revolution" in marriage. This fact calls for rethinking our approaches to marriage and redesigning our strategy to meet the new needs.

A survey of a cross-section of the U.S. adult population revealed these significant facts:*

1) Marriage is still very much "in"; 80 percent rank "a happy home life" at the top of their list of goals.

2) Marriage itself, rather than parenting, is central; three out of four persons felt it was all right for married couples to decide to have no children.

3) The majority approved changes in life-style such as leaving the work force temporarily, joining a new religion, moving to the country.

4) A slight majority of women (51 percent) and a somewhat larger majority of men (58 percent) support "woman's liberation," and this support is rising rapidly.

Since this survey covered all adult ages, let's look now at just the young adults. A study by Arlo Compaan of young adult couples in California reported:†

1) The husband-wife relationships tended to be emotionally intense and this relationship, rather than children, dominated the marriages.

2) Marriage was understood and valued mainly in terms of communication, personal growth, and satisfaction.

3) The couples preferred small families.

4) Play, including playful sex, was a stronger motif in marriage than production, the work ethic, or marriage as an aid to "success."

5) Religion was highly valued but the couples generally lacked interest in the church even though they were nominally "church related."

Let me add my observations concerning recent changes in marriage which affect all ages but are most prominent among young adults:

1) There's a growing search for more flexible, creative marriage styles.

2) The strongest single trend is a rejection of rigidly defined sex roles and a movement toward increasingly egalitarian man-woman relationships.

3) There's increasing willingness to consider options other than marriage and to be in much less hurry to marry.

4) "Just living together" without a marriage is becoming more common among couples who aren't ready for marriage or don't want legal commitments.

5) There's increased openness to the possibility of terminating a marriage if it proves not to be mutually fulfilling, and less of the "til death do us part" attitude.

6) There's more divorce and more remarriage.

7) The pill, equality, and freedom of women have narrowed dramatically and may eliminate the male-female dual standards on sex; there is generally more sexual freedom and variety before and within marriage.

8) There is a continuing decrease in the nurture and emotional support available to couples from their extended family and neighborhoods, and increased searching for substitute support systems—for example, in communes, family networks, and group marriages.

A New Strategy for a New Day

It's obvious that it's a whole new day for marriage—particularly among many young adults! What should be the response of the church to this challenge? The deep changes in marriage practices and attitudes make it imperative to develop a more effective methodology and program to help couples find what they want and need. Any new approach must help couples learn how to keep on enriching their marriage, so they can create flexible, growing, intensified monogamy, with a more enjoyable and soul-satisfying bond of creative closeness. It is precisely at the point of developing such a program that the use of growth counseling is most helpful.

Such a program needs two complementary parts: (1) enrichment groups, including seminars, workshops, retreats, and classes for all couples who want them, and (2) growth-centered crisis counseling for couples going through periods of special stress. The goal of both parts is to make good marriages better. Couples with acutely and chronically disturbed marriages should of course be helped to find specialists in longer-term marriage therapy.

I suggest that you read the following list to get a grasp of the immense variety and range of possibilities for marriage enrichment groups. Don't let the length of the list scare you. I'm not suggesting that your church should develop all or even most of these groups! That's probably neither necessary nor feasible. But churches that are using a growth model of ministry do devote major leadership energies to developing a variety of time-limited groups, retreats, and training seminars to meet major concentrations of needs. The goal is to gradually create a smorgasbord of enrichment and counseling opportunities to meet the needs of the maximum number of persons at all stages of marriage. Read the list with your particular situation in mind. Ask yourself whether or not there are unmet needs to which you could address yourself in one or more of these areas.

Types of Marriage Enrichment and Growth Counseling Groups and Programs

Youth identity-formation or self-discovery groups; long-range preparation for marriage

Preparation-for-marriage retreats or growth groups several times a year

Growth-oriented prewedding preparation sessions with each couple

Newly-marrieds enrichment workshop or retreat or growth group

Postwedding marriage enrichment sessions with each couple (at least two or three sessions)

Young parents enrichment group

Annual marriage enrichment retreats for couples clubs and classes

Preparation for baptism (or infant dedication) group for parents

Regular marriage enrichment retreats (for various ages and stages)

A creative sexuality seminar

A workshop on "Handling Conflict Creatively"

A Bible study—marriage enrichment workshop or class

A couples spiritual-discovery group

Meaning-of-life groups for couples

A middle-marrieds enrichment retreat

A parents-teens communication workshop

An emptying nest marriage enrichment group

Women's (or men's or mixed) consciousness-raising retreat

Family clusters or networks as a context for family enrichment

A creative values group or retreat

Healthy family growth celebrations, to make good families better

Divorce growth groups

Creative singlehood groups

Single parents enrichment groups

Creative retirement couples group

Grief recovery groups (for widows and widowers)

Growth group leadership training workshop

Growth training for teachers, and for leaders of youth and adult groups

A growth-oriented program of crisis counseling for couples

A growth group for couples after marriage counseling

The Goal

What is the goal of growth marriage counseling/enrichment? It's to provide the opportunity for each couple to create their own best marriage, a growing relationship that meets their needs. I'll call this kind of relationship—the kind that stimulates growth—an intimate, open marriage with equality and positive fidelity. The goal is a liberating marriage, one which frees couples to use their maximum gifts as individuals in mutually enhancing ways. Each couple develops its own variations on this theme.

The characteristics of a liberating marriage (described in *The Intimate Marriage** and *The Open Marriage*† include: responsiveness to meeting each other's needs; open and caring communication; closeness *and* respect for individual privacy needs; autonomy (each a person in his/her own right) *and* interdependence; genuine fairness and equality; commitment to each other's growth; no rigid or satellite roles; continued change and growth through the years; the ability to use conflict to deepen intimacy and resolve differences by negotiation (rather than deadlocking or distancing); deepening sexual pleasure integrated with love; increasing intimacy in the areas of meanings and faith; strengthening of the marriage identity (the "two becoming one").

In contrast to the position expressed in *The Open Marriage,* it is my conviction that, for most couples, *positive* fidelity is essential if they are to achieve "deepening sexual pleasure integrated with love." This is the integration which makes possible the most satisfying sex. *Negative* fidelity is a sexual faithfulness based mainly on guilt and fear of consequences. This is the control and punishment effected by one's internal "Parent," to use the PAC terms of Transactional Analysis.‡ Positive fidelity, in contrast, flows from mutual respect and caring and from prizing what the couple already have "going for them" and what they expect to build together. Sexual fidelity stems from a more inclusive "Adult" fidelity—from a valuing of, and commitment to, the relationship and from not wanting to damage what is experienced as precious. Negative fidelity, which feels like a moral straight jacket, is less and less prevalent or motivating, particularly among young adult couples.

Positive fidelity doesn't preclude the possibility of having close friends of the opposite sex. As we learn to relate to each other *first* as persons and *then* as sex objects, rather than vice versa, this becomes increasingly possible. Positive fidelity doesn't rule out the wandering eye or imagination, both of which seem to be normal, enjoyable aspects of our human sexuality. Positive fidelity is based on respecting a psychological reality—namely, that the most body and soul satisfying sex isn't possible apart from a quality of relationship which includes mutual respect, trust, tender caring, and continuity. It takes time and trust and commitment for love to flower. Affairs, rather than enhancing the quality of marriages, usually hurt them, often in irreparable ways. I'm all for an "open marriage" in terms of communication, equality, growth, and outside friendships. But if "open" means sexual affairs, the results are usually not openness or growth—or really liberating sex!

The deepest intimacy and the best sex of which most couples are capable are not possible psychologically apart from genuine equality. The distance and anger (whether hot or frozen) that build up in a one-up/one-down marriage in which one or both persons feel "used," block depth communication and therefore impede liberated sex. The awareness that we men also are exploited—by the present "success" system—and that we're also depriving ourselves of much of our personhood (by the male rat race) makes it obvious that the basic issue is *human* liberation. The goal is to create relationships and institutions in which both women and men will have the greatest freedom and encouragement to use their full intelligence, creativity, and productive energies. We who are married can help to overcome sexism, the prejudice and discrimination against women most obviously, but also against men, which blocks human becoming on a massive scale. We can do this by struggling, and by bearing the pain it often requires, to create an equal and mutually-liberating relationship.

In liberating our marriages we give our children a precious gift, the model of a mutually-fulfilling man-woman relationship, which is one of the best preparations for their future. The accelerating trend toward female-male equality opens up all sorts of new possibilities for both conflict and intimacy.

Sexism is a central cause of both diminished marriages and destructive marriages. Therefore, a church cannot fully nurture the growth of married persons until it actively encourages liberating, equal, intimate marriages. This will require deep changes in the institutional male chauvinism of most churches and religions. Until this happens, our effectiveness in marriage enrichment will be limited because of the spiritual destructiveness of the mutual exploitation which results from inequality. And not until this happens will we take seriously the insight of Paul that in Christ there is no male or female (Gal. 3:28), that one's *humanity,* not one's gender, is what matters most. The most important implication of all this is that marriage counselors and enrichers, whether ministers or lay persons, need to have increased awareness—a raised consciousness in the area of women's and men's liberation!

The Widening Impact of Marriage Enrichment

A minister asked during a workshop: "With the moral morass of our society, the stinking injustice at home, and the poverty and hunger all over the world, how can we spend time enriching marriages?" Anyone with a sensitive social conscience must find an answer. Let's face it—the human family may *not* make it. It may do itself in, sooner than most of us think, by massive environmental pollution, and/or a nuclear holocaust. And even if we make it, the quality of life may be reduced severely. Is it ethically responsible then to spend time enriching marriages—mainly among the affluent—when millions live in dehumanizing squalor, hunger, and disease?

For me, the answer is no—not if enrichment ends with individual marriages in a kind of mutual marital narcissism. Privatized, self-serving marriage enrichment, like privatized, self-serving religion and counseling, is immoral in our kind of world. It is an opiate which helps us ignore the massive social

injustices and economic inequalities which block the fulfillment of the God-given potentialities of millions of our brothers
and sisters on Spaceship Earth.

But, as pointed out earlier, to be genuinely liberating and
person-creating, marriage enrichment should produce commitment to outreach beyond the marriage! Enrichment of individual marriages is potentially a powerful resource for enriching life in society. The impact can be like a pebble dropped in
a pond. The first circle beyond the marriage pair is the immediate family. Parents are the architects and builders of a family; whatever makes their marriage better will strengthen the
personality health of their children. The outreach of enriched
couples can help build a network of mutual support among
families. This gradually strengthens the wholeness-sustaining
fabric of a congregation and community. Couples who have
mutually-satisfying marriages have the inner resources to
reach out to even wider circles. They can be challenged to
work in projects to improve their community through political
and social action, to help eradicate sexism, racism, ageism (discrimination against aging persons), and poverty, all of which
damage marriages and families. As responsible members of
the human family, we all should support governmental, United
Nations, and church-sponsored efforts to help families in poor
nations acquire the food, shelter, medical help, and education
which will allow them to use their full God-given potentialities.

Leaders of marriage enrichment events need to hold up outreach as indispensable to personal growth. The life-style of
"generativity" (Erik Erikson)—investing self in others and the
ongoingness of humankind—is essential to having the best
marriages at any stage.*

All this has deep roots in the Christian heritage. As John
Snow, a professor of pastoral theology, points out, the Christian family was seen in the New Testament as an agent of the
coming community of love and justice, a new kind of "kingdom": "Its goal was not to make a house a home for a family
but to make the world a home for humankind."†

> The family was not simply a way for two people of different
> sexes to meet each other's needs and the needs of their chil-

dren. It was part of a community committed to meeting the deprivation of the world, spiritual and physical. As such, marriage had the rich spiritual and emotional support of the community in which it existed.*

Today, Snow declares, the local church should provide the community of caring which is essential for healthy marriages and families. The ultimate goal of Christian marriage enrichment is to liberate couples to claim and share the fruits of the spirit for which the human family longs—love, faithfulness, integrity, reconciliation, healing, joy, and peace. When this happens, people discover the growth that comes only when one is captured by a commitment to helping others grow, and to creating a growth-supporting world community!

4. Relationship-Building Tools

The elements [of a dialogical relationship] are, first, a relation . . . between two persons, second, an event experienced
by them in common, . . . and third, the fact that this one
person, without forfeiting anything of the felt reality of his
activity, at the same time lives through the common event
from the standpoint of the other.*   —Martin Buber

The most satisfying and most complete example of ego transcendence, and certainly the most healthy from the point of
view of avoiding illness of the character, is the throwing of
oneself into a healthy love relationship.†
                                          —Abraham Maslow

The central task in both marriage enrichment and marriage
growth counseling, is to help couples enhance their dialogical
communication skills so they can nurture their love and resolve their conflicts constructively. What counts is the actual
practice of new communication skills. And being coached by
a counselor or group facilitator is the most efficient way to
learn to use them.

What follows are communication and relationship-building
tools which I have found useful in both couple counseling and
marriage enrichment groups. The best way to learn to use
them, and simultaneously to enhance your own communication skills, is to experience them. So, invite your spouse (or
any close friend) to join you as you try them. There's no
"right" or "wrong" way of experiencing any of these methods.
Your actual experience of them, however, affords your best
opportunity to increase your ability to communicate. Improving communication with others begins by enhancing communication within ourselves. In the first two exercises have someone read the instructions, stopping as long as necessary at each
slash (/) for you to do what has been suggested.

Strengthening Self-Awareness

Find a comfortable position; close your eyes to concentrate on your inner experience./

Center down; become aware of your body in this moment./

Breathe deeply several times, letting your tension go out as you exhale./

Picture your inner space, your consciousness, as a room within your mind. What kind of room is is? How is it furnished? How does it feel inside your consciousness?/

If your room feels cramped, enlarge your inner space by pushing back the walls—give your spirit more room./

Stay with your awareness now as you experience the center from which you relate./

Open your eyes and share your experience with your partner (or your group)./

Experiencing Inner Liberation

Developing a mutually liberating marriage depends, in part, on the degree to which we are free spirits. We project our feelings of trappedness or freedom onto our intimate relationships. This guided meditation focuses on inner liberation, and on our power to choose to be free within ourselves.

Get comfortable, close your eyes; center down, claiming your inner space./

Picture yourself inside a closed box./

Push on the sides to experience being boxed-in./

Examine your box, looking for a way out./

If you find a way, get out now./

If you're still in the box, invite whomever you need to help you out now./

See yourself in a beautiful spring meadow, enjoying its freedom and openness. Let yourself go!/

Be aware of differences between your feelings in the box and your feelings in the meadow./

If you're alone, invite someone to enjoy the meadow with you./

What in your actual life is represented by the particular box and meadow which you created?/

Return in your thoughts to where you're presently meeting, and share whatever you experienced with your spouse (or small group)./

What biblical themes come to your mind as you reflect on your box and meadow experience?/

Share these with each other./

This meditation goes to the heart of growth counseling—inner liberation leading to liberating relationships and ultimately to liberating institutions. I find I spend too much time in my box and not enough time in the inner freedom of my meadow. But this is my choice and I have the power to change it! How about you? Discuss this now./

Listening Responsively

Learning to listen sensitively, staying on the other's feeling wavelength, is a vital marital skill that can be strengthened by practice. Facing each other, one person simply states what he/she is feeling and experiencing *right now*. The partner listens carefully, and every few sentences, summarizes what was communicated both verbally and nonverbally, beginning with the words, "Do I hear you saying (or feeling). . . ?" Use no other questions or responses. Just try to understand the other's inner world; let that person know you are trying to understand, and keep checking to see how accurate your understanding is. Do this now./

Now reverse roles and let the other partner practice the responsive listening./

In workshops, two couples can work together taking turns coaching each other in listening more effectively. In counseling, the procedure can be used like this: "John, would you tell your wife how you feel about this?" Then (after he does so): "Mary, tell your husband what you heard him say, just to make sure you understand each other."

Affirming Our Strengths

Growth counseling helps couples become more aware of the assets in themselves and in their marriage. These methods are "hope awakeners":

Affirming Our History

Think back and recall two of your happiest experiences together. Relive these briefly in your memory./

Tell your spouse about your memory experiences./

Recall two difficult or bad times which you handled well; be aware of the strengths it took to cope constructively./

Share your memory trips, affirming your strengths from both the good times and the bad times./

Giving Gifts

Be a gift giver—tell your spouse all the things that you regard as his or her major assets, strengths, and attractive qualities./ The recipient should respond in terms of how those assets might be used more fully./

Now, reverse the process. (In a small group each person takes a turn at receiving the "gifts" from the other members.)/

Sharing Strengths

Take turns (in couples or in small groups) sharing something that made you feel especially good about yourself during the past two weeks./

Take turns sharing something that was heavy or painful to bear./

Now discuss how you feel about sharing recent joys and pain with each other./

Risking and Trusting

Here are some experiences for getting in touch with the trust/mistrust feelings so crucial in marriage:

Trust Jogging

Take turns leading each other for ten minutes each, with the one who is led being blindfolded; include at least two minutes of jogging./

Discuss what you learned about trusting each other./

Risking

Turn to your spouse and both talk gibberish (nonsense sounds) for one minute—risk appearing foolish, stupid, not in control./

Share your feelings about this./

Tell your spouse two secrets that will make him/her feel good./

Discuss why you had not risked telling these secrets before./

Evaluating Our Working Values

Value conflicts often go unrecognized and create blocked growth and pain in many marriages! Understanding each other's values, caring deeply about some of the same things and respecting the spouse's right to differ on other things— all help keep a marriage growing. Here are two exercises which can be used to help couples clarify and revise their values in two crucial areas in marriage:

Evaluating Our Time Priorities

Close your eyes and relax./

Imagine you've just been told that you have a limited amount of time in your marriage before one of you dies. How do you feel about this?/

What changes will you make in your present schedule and life-style in order to use the remaining time for the most important things? After a few minutes, open your eyes and share your experience with your partner./

If you experienced depressing or anxious feelings, these can be constructive pain—the pain of facing your finitude. Facing the fact that all of us *do* have a limited amount of time can make our lives together more precious. This exercise has helped some couples decide to spend more time together and less on the treadmill.

Evaluating Our Money Priorities

Close your eyes. Imagine that you have received a windfall of $15,000, the only condition being that you must spend it within two weeks./

Decide how you'll spend it./

Open your eyes and each of you jot down your list of expenditures, without comparing notes./

Now, compare your list with that of your spouse, discussing your assumptions about what's important—the values which guided your decisions./

Increasing Spiritual Intimacy

Continuing growth in the dimension of personal faith, in experiences of transcendence and in one's sense of relatedness to God and creation, is important in both marriage counseling and enrichment. Spiritual enrichment can well be the integrating center of marriage enrichment programs. Here are some ways to help couples communicate and grow in this area:

Drawing Your Theology

Take a piece of paper and a box of crayons./

Without planning what you'll do, express your feelings about God (or the Bible, or religion, or the church). Do it quickly. Let your fingers express freely how you really feel about these matters./

Share your drawing with your spouse, discussing its meaning./

Paraphrasing Biblical Passages

Working as a couple, read 1 Corinthians 13 (or another passage) and write out a paraphrase (in your own words) in terms of your own marriage./

Share your paraphrases with your group./

Doing Theology

Our personal theology includes our guiding principles for living and relating. Each of you write out a list of insights from the Bible that you find realistic and meaningful in your marriage./

See if you can combine your list and that of your spouse into a joint theology of your marriage./

Celebrating the Gifts of Marriage

After struggle, pain, and growth together in a counseling session or enrichment event, it's good to lift up, in a brief worship happening, the gifts of the Creator which have been experienced together. Celebrate now whatever you have experienced in using these growth tools: move beyond communicating *about* the experience to the deeper sharing which is communion.

Enhancing Sexual Enjoyment

Many couples can improve their sex life and rekindle romance by methods such as the following:

Creating a More Sensual Setting for Lovemaking

Devise and implement a plan to do this—for example, by adding candlelight, mood music, a waterbed, a "childproof" lock on the bedroom door, or finding a secluded meadow or beach.

Cultivating the Art of Mutual, Nondemand Pleasuring

Give each other a leisurely, full-body massage, using warm body lotion. Just relax and enjoy it. Flow with the pleasure wherever it takes you. Don't worry about "making it" or get caught in the "we try harder" syndrome. Enjoy receiving and giving sensual pleasure. Sex *is* one of God's best gifts—so enjoy it leisurely and lustily.

Telling Each Other Exactly What You Enjoy Most

While you're pleasuring or "making love" try signaling by sounds, words, or gestures which words, caresses, smells, motions, positions, or love-play you find most stimulating, and when you're ready to climax. It's very much to each person's advantage to guide the other in maximizing pleasuring!

Reconnecting Regularly

Sex is communication—an intense form of communication! It improves as other communication bridges between you are strengthened. Spend some time together each day seeking to get reconnected through communicating, caring, affirming each other, and dealing with small hurts and frictions that otherwise may build into a cold wall that blocks the flow of loving, sensual feelings.

Letting Your "Child" Side Play Regularly

Try scheduling mini-vacations at least once a week—times away from the things that keep your inner "Parent" (the responsible, work-oriented, "don't enjoy" side) activated. Some couples swap baby-sitting to assure themselves time together away from their children. Letting your fun-loving side frolic regularly refills the inner springs and also enlivens sex. "Unless you become like a little child . . . ."

Coping Constructively with Conflict

In marriage and premarriage enrichment events and in crisis counseling it's important to help couples become more skillful in handling the conflict and anger that are normal in any close relationship. Here are some methods that help:

Scheduling Regular Times for Clearing the Air

Minor annoyances, hurt feelings, and conflicts can grow into major problems. At appointed intervals, at least weekly, bring them out and articulate them. We try to do this on Wednesdays at our house, so that we can enjoy our more relaxed weekend opportunities for intimacy. The biblical wisdom about not letting the sun go down on your anger (Eph. 4:26) is salutary for marriages.

Discovering Physical Ways to Release Pent-Up Frustration

Beat the pillow or pound the bed with fists or a tennis racket, or kick a cardboard carton, until the held-in feelings are released and drained off. Or, as a couple, a few rounds of harmless pillow-fighting or Indian arm wrestling—with the stronger person using his/her weaker arm to equalize the struggle—can help bring repressed negative feelings to the surface where they can be dealt with.

Negotiating No-Lose Compromise Solutions

Keep your inner Adult in control during negotations. See to it that in such negotiations each person's needs are met to some extent. The heart of any conflict is a collision between the needs/wants of the two persons. In a marriage, if one "wins" and the other "loses" *both* lose because the relationship is hurt.* The Intentional Marriage Method (see above pp. 10–17) is a method of positive conflict prevention and Adult-to-Adult conflict resolution. Couples who have learned how to use the Parent/Adult/Child aspect of Transactional Analysis (see p. 81, n. 23‡) have a tool for conflict resolution and for employing the IMM more effectively.

Other Sources of Marriage-Building Tools

Additional tools for enrichment groups and growth counseling are plentifully available.* However, I recommend that you develop your own repertoire or growth tools, learning from others, adapting and creating your own.

5. Retreats and Groups

> When I am coming alive I know that I am coming alive. The cosmic covenant means coming into living harmony with the self, the universe, and God.*　　　　　—Mary Daly

> Man can become whole not in virtue of a relation to himself but only in virtue of a relation to another self. This other self may be just as limited and conditioned as he is; in being together the unlimited and the unconditioned is experienced.†
> 　　　　　　　　　　　　　　　　　　—Martin Buber

The heart of a church's marriage growth program is its enrichment retreats, workshops, and groups. Marriage enrichment events are the best means of attracting the maximum number of couples who want to "make good marriages better." They do this by learning to nurture their love and become part of a caring community of couples supporting each other's growth. Enrichment events offer the best way to discover persons who are natural growth facilitators. With additional training and coaching, these lay persons can lead effective enrichment groups. Marriage enrichment events also encourage couples with deadlocked or deeply hurting marriages to gain enough hope to seek marriage counseling, often sooner than they otherwise would. Such events after counseling help couples continue the growth they began in counseling.

In marriage enrichment workshops—I'll use "workshop" interchangeably with "retreat"—and groups, it's well to blend four types of activities: (1) Whole group communication exercises and brief input sessions to share practical ideas, for example, about Transactional Analysis or sex. (2) Couple activities, especially relationship-building experiences such as the Intentional Marriage Method. Many couples find the times they spend together doing their marriage "growth work" the most valuable part of a workshop or group. One man stated, after a one-day workshop, "The most useful aspect was the opportunity to be together with my partner and discuss feelings, wants, and needs, and possible solutions. Excellent opportunity to revitalize our paths of communication and appreciation for each other!" (3) Small, usually leaderless sharing groups of three or four couples into which the membership of an entire workshop is divided. These small groups can often be meaningful and effective in encouraging each other's growth. (4) Relaxation and fun periods, both planned and "free time," are essential during intensive retreats to keep the struggles of growth work from becoming a drag, and to encourage growth in that playfulness which keeps sparkle in a marriage. We often shortchange this aspect in retreats because of our "workaholic" tendencies.

Some Basic Ingredients

Here are some ingredients—themes which I often include in enrichment events, depending on the length of the period and the interests of the group. Those preceded by a dagger are included in nearly every group:

†Getting Connected as a Group and as Couples

I open a group workshop by discussing the possibilities of marriage enrichment events. Couples then are asked to talk as couples for a few minutes about their hopes and expectations for the experience. Then I ask the group to say what they hope to get from the experience (listing these needs on newsprint). Through group discussion the major goals, topics, and agenda items are then chosen, in light of the group's needs and what the leaders and the group offer to meet these needs. This process ("developing a group contract") is essential for any growth event, since all real learning-growing is motivated by the participants' needs and interests. The needs of most couples groups cluster around the topics listed below.

†Strengthening Our Communication Skills

This is needful and helpful both in the total group and later in the small groups. Self-awareness and responsive listening exercises (see above pp. 29–30) need continuing emphasis throughout a group. Schedule several communication-building experiences near the beginning to build group rapport, reduce initial anxieties, and give couples the immediate satisfaction of learning useful skills.

†Affirming Our Strengths and Building Trust

Schedule this for couples and small groups (see above pp. 30–32) *before* dealing with anxiety-laden issues such as conflict resolution, changing roles, crisis coping, or sex.

†Using the Intentional Marriage Method

This is the "heart" of our workshops (see above pp. 10–17). The process involves couples working separately and then coming together in sharing groups for debriefing.

†Approaching Conflict Through Role Playing

The use of role playing to act out a marriage conflict chosen by the whole group can help couples learn to use Transactional Analysis as a practical tool (see above pp. 35–36, 70).

†Discovering Creativity in Changing Roles

Work first with the whole group, then with small groups, helping couples handle the conflict and discover the creativity made possible by the emerging, more fulfilling women-men identities. Begin with inner liberation (see above pp. 29–30), then discuss paths to human liberation and a liberating marriage.

Enhancing Sexual Enjoyment

The aim here is to brighten dull romance by encouraging sex-affirmative attitudes and nondemand pleasuring, pleasure enjoyed for its own sake without any other goal or expectation of achievement. Schedule free time for couples, after discussions of pleasuring, to have private "lab sessions," to practice massage, etc., in their own rooms (see above pp. 34–35).

†Evaluating Our Values

Beginning with couples, then sharing groups, help couples to become aware of the implicit values which guide their choices, to look at the consequences of these choices, and then to determine whatever changes in priorities and values are needed for improving the quality of their lives (see above p. 32).*

†Deepening Spiritual Intimacy

Proceeding from the whole group to small groups to couples, focus on values and on ways to encourage each other's continuing spiritual development, resolve religious conflicts, increase "peak experiences" in marriage, celebrate our struggles and growth together, and deepen experiences of nurturing trust in the Spirit of life and love (see above p. 33).

Coping With Crises in Marriage

With the whole group and the small groups, focus on learning skills which couples can use to help themselves and others experience crises as incentives for growth (see below pp. 64–66).

Enriching Parent-Child and Parent-Youth Relations

Help the whole group and the small groups to focus on growth approaches to parenting, and how parent roles can enrich or impoverish marriages.† Discuss the enrichment of marriages without children.

Examining Growth Possibilities in Marriage Stages

Invite the whole group and then also the small groups to examine the problems and potentials of the stage or stages of the participants—for example, premarriage, newly-married (pre-children), the young-children years, middle-years stage I (parents of teens); middle-years stage II (empty nest); the retirement years.‡

†Raising the Enjoyment Quotient

Relaxation and fun periods may just happen. But they should also be scheduled: relaxation sessions, moving to music, volleyball, group shoulder rub in a circle (an excellent waker-upper when things begin to drag), trust jog, free time to "do your own thing," etc.

†Developing Intimacy Through Outreach

Couples can be helped to discover—often to their surprise —their potential as marriage enrichers. They can increase the outreach dimension of marriage by developing a "couple investment plan"—a strategy for responding to particular marriage and family needs in the congregation and community. Practicing generativity is the way to avoid group and family "in-grown-itis."

†Contracting for Continuing Growth

Before the end of a group or workshop, give couples an opportunity to develop their "growth covenant"—concrete next steps they will take toward their growth goals—and let them share this with the group. The entire group should also formulate plans to provide continuing mutual growth support to each other. Follow-up meetings can make a decisive difference in encouraging continued growth, when the going gets rough for individual couples.

†Evaluating the Experience

At the close of any group or workshop, invite persons to complete briefly and in writing these statements: (1) The most helpful parts of this group were. . . . (2) The least helpful or unhelpful were. . . . (3) My overall evaluation is. . . . (4) On the basis of this experience, I now plan to. . . . (5) My suggestions for future groups are. . . . Halfway through a workshop, a midstream evaluation is also useful, as is a five-minute evaluation period at the end of each meeting of an ongoing group.

†Closing the Group or Retreat

It's important for persons to learn the skills of closing a chapter in their experience by facing their feelings about it—including grief feelings—celebrating what has been, and affirming each other for the gift of sharing. A worship moment at the end of a group session (for example, sentence prayers in a circle of joined hands) or a fuller closing to end an intensive workshop can heighten awareness of the transcendent dimension in all genuine relating and growth. At the end of an intensive group it is well to point out that something of a letdown is natural after any mountain-peak experience.

Sample Schedules

Here are sample schedules for three enrichment models which we have found to be effective in connection with the basic ingredients listed above:

Model I. A One-Day Retreat

A Saturday retreat with two to four weekly follow-up sessions can be effective with twelve, twenty-four, or even forty-eight couples if the co-leaders provide meaningful structures for the whole group and for the small groups and couple sharing.

8:30 A.M.—Couples gather, have coffee, chat, make name tags, and on their tags draw a symbol to communicate their hopes for the event.

8:45 A.M.—Getting connected and establishing group contract (in a circle).

9:15 A.M.—Exercise to strengthen communication and affirm our strengths (see above pp. 29–31).

10:00 A.M.—Coffee break.

10:20 A.M.—The Intentional Marriage Method.

11:50 A.M.—Evaluating the morning. Singing a folk hymn while joining hands in a circle.

12:00 NOON—Lunch, with the small groups eating together, each perhaps at its own table. Free time.

The choice of afternoon topics is influenced by the particular interests of the group.

12:45 P.M.—Trust jog or something else with lively movement.

1:10 P.M.—A lively, experiential topic, such as resolving conflict (using role playing) or changing roles.

2:10 P.M.—Coffee break.

2:30 P.M.—A film such as "Sexuality and Communication"* followed by co-leaders dialogue on enhancing sexual pleasure.

3:50 P.M.—Sing a song or do a mutual shoulder rub.

4:00 P.M.—Evaluating our working values experientially (in small groups); leads into a discussion of couple investment plans and outreach.

4:50 P.M.—Planning follow-up, by couples and then as a group.

5:15 P.M.—Closing worship, celebrating our sharing and affirming our plans for the future.

5:25 P.M.—Evaluating the day; group discussion and written evaluations.

Intensive workshops leave people tired but exhilarated. I am impressed with the significant progress many couples make in even eight hours of growth work.

One participant wrote in her evaluation: "Beneficial! Just hope we can continue to have our skills grow. Because I was the one who suggested coming, and my husband seemed to get so much out of it, it was doubly worthwhile." Another wrote: "A most rewarding day, to be with my wife, and to share fellowship with others we didn't know before but to be together as a family in the sharing."

It's well to recommend that couples plan to have dinner out after a retreat to close the day with fun. Follow-up sessions, beginning a week later, build on the growth work begun at the retreat.

Model 2. A Weekend Retreat

A three-day retreat with one to three follow-up sessions can be effective for twelve, twenty-four, or even forty-eight couples.

Friday

6:00 P.M.—Couples gather for supper, get acquainted, sing.

7:00 P.M.—Getting connected; establishing group contract.

7:45 P.M.—Awareness-communication exercises.

8:15 P.M.—Sharing groups. Form a sharing group with three other couples you'd like to get better acquainted with this weekend./

Discuss what you learned by this process of self selection./

Tell each person in your group something you like about him or her./

Discuss this experience./

9:00 P.M.—Close your eyes; imagine you're standing in front of each person in your group, one at a time, saying to each one in turn, "I need you."/

Share your inner experience with your group./

9:30 P.M.—Evaluate the first session. Close with a brief worship event including joining hands in a circle and affirming the persons on both sides of you as children of God, using the nonverbal language of your hands. Sing "Shalom," remembering that the word means wholeness or fulfillment as well as peace.

Free time; informal fellowship.

Saturday

8:00 A.M.—Song and breakfast.

8:40 A.M.—Communication exercise: responsive listening with two couples working together.

9:30 A.M.—Coffee break.

9:45 A.M.—The IMM.

10:45 A.M.—Sharing groups; check out IMM plans.

11:30 A.M.—Risking and trust exercises.

12:15 P.M.—Evaluating the morning. Holding hands in a circle, sing the table blessing.

12:30 P.M.—Lunch.

1:00-3:00 P.M.—Free time for couple communication while sitting on a rock in the sun, hiking, etc.

3:00-6:00 P.M.—Topics chosen by the group, such as conflict resolution, changing roles, coping with crises, parent-child relations. Approach these experientially, using guided fantasies, role playing, group discussion, etc.

6:00 P.M.—Supper.

7:00 P.M.—Enhancing sex.

8:30 P.M.—Letting our Child sides play: informal party; refreshments.

Sunday

8:00 A.M.—Breakfast.

8:30 A.M.—Sing a folk hymn.

Theme for the morning: "Experiencing the Good News in Our Marriages."

Evaluating our values, as couples and then in sharing groups.

Experiencing the caring community, in small groups. Each person shares something that causes him/her joy or pain (see above p. 31).

Experiencing truth from our heritage. Couples write paraphrases of 1 Corinthians 13 as this passage relates to their experience with the IMM on Saturday. They discuss next steps in their growth. Then they share this experience with their small group.

11:10 A.M.—Celebrating our relationships; experiential worship planned by group members.

Theme: "The greatest of these. . . ." Increasing our awareness of the Source of the love we know in our marriages. Couples share what has been spiritually meaningful during retreat. Closing: communion or love feast using the symbols of God's nurturing love. Spouses give each other the elements.

11:45 A.M.—Planning group follow-up sessions and outreach expressions.

12:15 P.M.—Oral and written evaluations of the retreat.

Concentrated enrichment weekends like this have significant impacts on many participants. Couples clubs and church school classes that hold such "growth boosters" annually report that the quality of their ongoing relationships and study is markedly enhanced.

Model 3. A Multiple Session Enrichment Group

A series of four to ten sessions can include a mini-retreat near the beginning. The four-hour mini-retreat intensifies relationships and builds trust which help to make the two-hour weekly sessions more productive. Since I have already discussed methods of facilitating growth groups and marriage enrichment groups earlier in this book and elsewhere* I won't repeat these here. Many of these can be useful in the weekly groups' sessions. Another effective approach, which is easier for leaders with limited experience, is to build sessions around book chapters which the couples agree to read together between meetings. For example, the chapters of our book *The Intimate Marriage* (hereafter referred to as *TIM*) can be used, with supplemental resources, in an eight-session enrichment group (the communication exercises at the end of each chapter can facilitate experiential learning and sharing).

Session 1. The Importance and Nature of Intimacy (Read

chaps. 1 and 2 in *TIM* before the session; begin by discussing how the ideas relate to your marriages.)

Session 2: Mutual Need Satisfaction and Communication (Read chaps. 4 and 5 in *TIM* as preparation.)

Session 3: (Mini-Retreat) The Intentional Marriage Method

Session 4: Barriers to Intimacy; Creative Conflict (Read chap. 3 in *TIM;* also chap. 1 of Bach and Wyden, *The Intimate Enemy.*)

Session 5: The Challenge of Changing Roles (Read chaps. 1-4 of *Meet Me in the Middle.**)

Session 6: Sexual Intimacy (Read chap. 7 in *TIM* and *The Joy of Sex.†*)

Session 7: Spiritual Intimacy (Read chap 9 in *TIM.*)

Session 8: Our Marriage and a Better World (Read chap. 10 in *TIM* and chap. 8 of *Meet Me in the Middle.*)

Optimal sized growth groups are five or six couples. Those who sign up should agree to attend all sessions unless prevented by some major unexpected event. Close the group to additional couples after the first or second session. Trust can't develop if the group changes constantly.

Recruiting Enrichment Groups

Ministers have quoted these statements by parishioners: "We don't need the marriage retreat—there's nothing wrong with our marriage!" "We don't believe in washing personal linen in public!" "I've heard about those sensitivity groups!" To diminish these three common, resistance-fostering fears, publicity on enrichment events should make clear that their purpose is to "make good marriages better" by discovering positive strengths and increasing here-and-now communication skills. State that the group is *not* marriage therapy or a "sensitivity" group (which often implies embarrassing self-revealing or hostility ventilation) but an opportunity to experience and increase Christian love in marriage. The family enrichment committee, which preplans the event with the pastor, should share responsibility for recruiting through announcements in church bulletins and personal contacts.

Other Considerations

It is highly desirable—particularly because of currently changing roles—to have male-female co-leaders in all marriage enrichment groups and events. Charlotte and I find that working together can be satisfying and good for our marriage, and frustrating, because of our areas of disagreement. When we're in a distancing cycle—that is, responding in ways that push each other further apart—we have to get reconnected ourselves before we can facilitate anyone else's growth.

For church groups, effective marriage enrichment retreats can occur in the church fellowship halls or lounges. This keeps the costs down, which is important particularly for many younger couples. The all-important ground rule is that everyone who enrolls agrees to attend all sessions. A more remote motel, retreat center, or church camp has certain advantages —advantages which may offset the usually higher costs. It allows people to slow down enough to collect themselves, center on the task, and take a fresh look at their marriages. Being away together for an intensive weekend of growth work and play often accelerates the process of awakening tired relationships (sexually and in other ways).

Before couples come to an enrichment event, encourage them to prepare by reading and discussing a book on growth approaches to marriage. For those who do this—and perhaps half of them will—this process primes the growth pump as they talk about their relationship, often more than they've ever done before. Other couples are inspired to read books on marriage after the event; this helps them continue their growth work.

At the close of an enrichment retreat, one man wrote on his evaluation: "Excellent experience—for me to really talk and listen to my wife—I can see the difference it will make in our day-to-day living. My overall evaluation—the best time we have had together in years!" Enrichment groups and workshops for couples can be launching pads which lift their marriage into continuing growth orbits. By using their new tools and continuing in a couple support group, their relationship can continue to grow through their years together.

6. Preparing for a Good Marriage

We *must* understand love; we must be able to teach it, to create it, to predict it, or else the world is lost to hostility and to suspicion.*   —Abraham Maslow

Marriage . . . will never be given new life except by that out of which true marriage always arises, the revealing by two people of the *Thou* to one another. Out of this a marriage is built up by the *Thou* that is neither of the *I's*.†
                                                               —Martin Buber

Ministers and congregations have a strategic opportunity to help couples prepare for good marriages. Yet, much so-called premarital counseling is of questionable effectiveness. Because many ministers are aware of this, they're searching for better approaches. The growth perspective provides a more workable and effective approach. It points to what is really appropriate and needed by the couple—not "counseling" (in the sense of dealing primarily with problems) but personalized training and coaching in relationship-building skills. Most couples are open to training which affirms their basic strengths and responds to their desire to develop the best possible marriage.

A Premarriage Growth Program

The minister and key lay persons—perhaps the marriage enrichment or family life committee—should develop a growth-oriented preparation-for-marriage program including a clear statetment of what is expected of couples. This plan should be discussed with the church's lay leaders, both women and men, to get their feedback and support. It can then be shared with the congregation through bulletins or newsletters at least twice a year. Thus the plan becomes generally known in the parish.

The plan should distinguish remote preparation for marriage from prewedding preparation. The former includes identity– and self-esteem–strengthening experiences for youth and opportunities to learn communication and relationship skills.

The prewedding phase of the program—which ideally builds on remote preparation experiences—should begin as long as possible before the "rush and crush" period, hopefully at least six months in advance of the wedding. Preparation crammed into the hectic few days preceding the ceremony is largely wasted, wiped out by anticipatory anxiety and fatigue. Such premarriage cram sessions may be the best that is possible with couples from out of town or outside the congregation. In such cases, a strong emphasis ought to be put on postwedding growth experience. Such cases, however, should increasingly be the exception to the generally followed longer-range preparation program. When I was a parish minister, I now realize, I should have been more emphatic in expecting couples to plan their wedding so as to include sound marriage preparation.

Some churches have developed brochures describing their premarriage programs and the mechanics of arranging for the wedding. Here are some things to include in such a brochure:

Getting a Head Start in Marriage
Marriage is what you make of it! Building a good marriage takes the loving skill of two persons who are willing to work —and play—at it to keep it growing! You undoubtedly want a fulfilling and happy marriage. Your minister and church stand behind you in this desire. A four-part program is available to help you get the best possible start in this demanding, exciting new chapter in your lives. Couples planning to be married in our church are expected to participate in all four parts, unless unusual circumstances make this impossible. As your pastor, let me emphasize that it's to your advantage to participate in all parts of the program.

First, participate in one of the preparation-for-marriage groups available three times a year in our church. Each group is open to a maximum of six couples planning marriage within the next year. You'll probably find you have a lot in common with the others. The focus will be on deepening communication, discovering the strengths in your relationship, and using these to develop the kind of mutually-satisfying marriage you both want. The dates for the next group are

———————. I suggest you sign up as early as possible by phoning me at ——————. I think you'll enjoy the experience.

Second, read and discuss as a couple these two books on building a good marriage: ——————————— and ————————————. You may borrow them from the church library if you wish. Couples report that this reading stimulates helpful conversations about their relationship.

Third, plan to meet with me as your pastor at least once or twice before the wedding to get better acquainted, discuss any concerns you have—perhaps as a result of your reading, group participation, or otherwise—and plan how your wedding can be made most meaningful to you. I'll look forward to these informal conversations. Phone me and we'll schedule them beginning, if possible, at least a month before the wedding. Note the dates and times of your scheduled sessions here: ——————; ——————; ——————. [One session may suffice for couples who have participated in an effective preparation for marriage group.]

Fourth, following the wedding, I would like to invite you to meet with me after three months, six months, and a year, to chat about how things are going as you experience new joys and pressures during the first year. Most couples find these sessions worthwhile. The date for your first postwedding meeting will be: ——————.

As you think about your busy schedule, this program may seem heavy to you. It *will* take time, but afterwards I think you'll feel that the time was well invested in your future happiness. I'm looking forward to being a part of this important milestone in your lives. Phone me if you have any questions.

Your Pastor

A Preparation-for-Marriage Group

Premarriage couples tend to be less strongly motivated than many married couples by a sense of need for enrichment. Therefore, a less demanding format for premarriage groups is likely to result in better participation. One California church held several well-attended marriage enrichment retreats, but a weekend premarriage retreat "fizzled" from lack of registration. This church subsequently has had well-attended and effective premarriage seminars meeting weekly for five evenings.

A church near a Midwest college had several growth groups "for anyone thinking about getting married," co-led by the pastor and his wife and meeting at the parsonage for six weekly sessions. A four-hour mini-marathon (for example, from 7:00-11:00 P.M.) near the beginning of a weekly pre-marriage series helps deepen group relationships and accelerate effective growth work by the couples.

Since as few as three couples can constitute a workable group, most churches can attract enough participants for two or three premarital groups a year. Or several churches can co-sponsor groups with teams of male-female co-leaders from among their ministers and laity. If a premarriage seminar or group must be larger than six couples, it's well to begin with brief seed-planting talks—for example, on resolving conflict, sex, men-women roles, values, and spiritual growth— and to follow these talks by three-couple sharing groups.

Whatever else occurs, it is essential to include communication exercises in which the couples can participate. The enrichment tools described in chapters 4 and 5 are useful in premarital groups. One important principle in all premarriage sessions is to focus mainly on things the people present have experienced: "In what areas do you find it difficult to communicate?" "How do you resolve the conflict when you disagree over something important?" "What are the major assets of your relationship?" This focus is more productive than speculating about what might happen after the wedding. It's also helpful to include a couple married less than five years as catalysts in premarriage groups.

A Sample Agenda

This sample agenda also gives some of the key topics to cover in premarriage groups and/or counseling:

Session 1. Two hours

Getting acquainted: Introduce your partner; tell how you met, recount your wedding plans, etc.

Male-female co-leaders dialogue on the purpose of the group; participants say what they expect and want from the group.

Co-leaders review principles for keeping marriages growing.

Couples experience the IMM, then discuss mutual need satisfaction.

Homework: Practice the IMM on your own; read an assigned book chapter.

Session 2. Four-hour mini-retreat

Share what you learned from the homework.

Communication skills: Practice responsive listening, using the PAC terminology and understandings of Transactional Analysis to strengthen Adult-to-Adult relating.

Resolving conflict constructively; role play a typical pre-marriage conflict.

Film: "Sexuality and Communication," followed by discussion on methods of enhancing sex.

Children: discussing whether to have or not? how many? their likely impact on our marriage; preparing for parenthood.

Homework: Take and score the Sex Knowledge Inventory*; discuss the experience. Read an assigned book chapter together.

Closing affirmation circle.

Session 3. Two hours

Feedback from homework. What did you learn from the Sex Knowledge Inventory?

The importance of our inner freedom and growth; use the box and meadow fantasy (see above pp. 29–30). Balance time together and time alone; respect each other's varying needs for closeness and for solitude and distance.

The impact of money issues on our relationship.

Homework: Take and score the Marriage Role Expectation Inventory†; compare your attitudes about what is "right" behavior for men and women in marriage.

Session 4. Two hours

How traditional or "liberated" are our inner role images? Changing roles and mutually-fulfilling marriages. Two-career marriages.

What does "holy matrimony" mean to you? Discuss the marriage ceremony in terms of a *relational or interpersonal theology.*

Invite couples to write their own services expressing their

own commitments, insights, and hopes, while eliminating sexism and such inequalities as the father giving the bride away.

Growth in spiritual intimacy and values in marriage.

The outreach to society in your marriage: avoiding ingrownness.

Finding your caring community: the church and your marriage.

Evaluating the four sessions: Plan for possible "reunions" of the group. Explain the importance of the postwedding conversations with the pastor. Set up one or more premarriage sessions for each couple.

Closing worship-celebration and affirmation circle.

Premarriage Growth Counseling with Couples

It helps both pastor and couples if these realistic goals of the prewedding sessions are clearly understood by both: (1) Building or strengthening the minister-couple relationship is the most important single goal! (2) Providing the couple—if they choose—opportunities to discuss problems or anxieties, and the pastor opportunities to provide personalized instruction relevant to their *felt* needs. This is called "educative counseling," and since I've discussed elsewhere its methods as applied to premarital interviews, I won't repeat them here.* (3) Affirming the couple by helping them recognize their strengths and assets; encouraging them to use these assets in developing a mutually-actualizing marriage. (4) Helping the couple plan and understand the wedding ceremony so that the experience will be for them a celebration of the *new reality they are creating*—their relationship! A wedding opens the door to *holy* matrimony if spiritual growth becomes real and ongoing in the marriage. (5) Setting up one or more postwedding sessions.

If a couple has participated in an enrichment group, the pastor can build on that by asking "What in the group experience was most important for your relationships?" If couples haven't been in a group, it's helpful to teach them the IMM and open up the topics listed in the sample agenda above. In either case, it's important to use the growth approach so that they do not feel "on trial" in any sense. Help them look at their problems in the context of their strengths and rich potentialities! The message to emphasize throughout premarital work is this: Your relationship probably is fulfilling in many ways already; it has many exciting additional possibilities which you can bring into fuller reality in your years together. Your church, through its growth group program, and your pastor, as friend and counselor, are your allies as you work to actualize these beautiful potentials.

Premarital Sex and "Living Together"

Since the research of Alfred Kinsey a generation ago, premarital intercourse has seemingly become much more widespread and acceptable in American society.* The changes are particularly striking among women, with a virtual abandonment of the dual standard. According to a recent national study,† by age twenty-five, 3/4 of all single women have had intercourse (as contrasted with 1/3 of Kinsey's sample). Males are beginning sex earlier: 3/4 of noncollege and 1/2 of college males (as compared with 2/3 and 1/4 respectively in Kinsey's study) have had intercourse by age seventeen.

What are the implications in these changes for premarital counseling? It's important for pastors to feel and to create a climate of acceptance of persons that respects their right to differ on sexual standards. This will free couples to discuss whatever positive or negative feelings they have. Many young people feel freer today to talk openly about sex and to practice sex, but this does not mean that they necessarily have accurate knowledge, constructive attitudes, or the capacity for full enjoyment. (The study cited above *does* show that the rate of orgasm has increased drastically among single women since Kinsey's time.)

In premarriage growth groups and counseling I usually begin a discussion of sex with, "I realize that you're probably well informed in this area but I make it a practice to review some basics so as not to miss important things. OK?" The minister's openness in discussing sex helps couples feel free to discuss whatever is on their minds. One shouldn't assume that couples who practice permissive approaches to sex either have or do not have the guilt feelings that the minister might have under similar circumstances.

Premarital sessions with couples who've been "living together" in a committed relationship have many similarities with marriage enrichment or counseling. If either or both have had previous "mini-marriages," problems similar to remarriage may be present—for example, unresolved feelings about the previous partners. Some persons fear that formalizing a relationship by a wedding will make them feel trapped. It's crucial to encourage them to discuss and work through such feelings. Couples who are living together may expect judgmentalism or put-downs from a minister. They'll be refreshed if instead they discover warm acceptance of them as persons, and a viewing of the past as prologue, as a foundation of valuable—though sometimes painful—experiences on which they can build!

The Pregnant Couple

If the minister knows a couple is pregnant, it's important to do several things during the premarriage sessions. Encourage them to explore whatever feelings they have about this fact—anxiety, blame, guilt, joy. Check to see if they're being pressured to marry—by either of them or by well-meaning but misguided parents. Help them evaluate their own readiness for marriage so that, if they're not ready, they can consider alternatives such as adoption or abortion. If you suspect that a couple is pregnant, try to create an opportunity for them to say openly whether they are, so that the issues can be discussed frankly. Otherwise their feelings about hiding this fact may alienate them from the minister and from that church after the wedding.

The affirming human potentials approach to premarriage work is never more salutary or important than when it is used with couples who feel self-criticism and guilt, or expect rejection by the minister. Surprise them with acceptance and affirmation!

7. Enriching a New Marriage

One of the deepest satisfactions coming from the healthy love relationship reported by my subjects is that such a relationship permits the greatest spontaneity, the greatest naturalness, the greatest dropping of defenses. . . . In such a relationship it is not necessary to be guarded, to conceal, to try to impress, to feel tense, to watch one's words or actions. . . . They can feel psychologically (as well as physically) naked and still feel loved and wanted and secure.* —Abraham Maslow

This fragile life between birth and death can nevertheless be a fulfillment—if it is a dialogue. In our life and experience we are addressed by thought and speech and action. . . . For the most part we do not listen.† —Martin Buber

Marriage Enrichment in the First Five Years

They are so precious—those early years of marriage! When our love is so young and our children so small! What a pity that so much of those years' potential is lost amidst unpaid bills and diaper pails, too little time together and too much scrambling for success. Helping couples during these years of learning-to-be-married is a critically important, but largely neglected, opportunity for churches.

Couples who have had optimal preparation, as described in chapter 6, can continue their growth in vigorous, imaginative programs for newly-marrieds. For the vast majority who have not been adequately prepared, such programs are even more vital. The aim is to help couples make the most of the early formative years and thus build strong foundations for lifelong patterns of creative relating.

A man in his middle years described his hopes for a weekend couples retreat: "I hope we can achieve that good, close feeling and learn to help others do better than we've done—we've wasted so much time in our marriage!" Life is so short, and it becomes very important to learn, in the early years, to use well the precious time we have in intimate relationships.

Here are six interrelated ways in which, through church counseling and enrichment programs, couples can strengthen their own new marriages. I present these models in the hope that they will stimulate your creativity, encouraging you to experiment until you discover the one or two models which work best in your situation.

Model I. Healthy Marriage Growth Interviews

The purposes and method of setting up a series of post-wedding growth sessions were presented in chapter 6. If a couple is moving after the wedding, the pastor who performed the ceremony should phone a minister in the new community asking him or her to take responsibility for the follow-up sessions. Newlyweds who move into your community after being married elsewhere should be encouraged to participate in the entire early-marrieds' program.

Healthy marriage interviews should be publicized as a regular important part of a church's enrichment program, using an announcement such as this:

> *Marriage Enrichment Sessions with Minister*
> Our church cares about helping persons at each marital stage to have satisfying marriages. The early years of marriage are usually a time of struggle and adjustment. Therefore, our pastor wants to have several informal "enrichment sessions" with each couple who desire this enrichment during their first two years. These sessions are opportunities for couples to discuss their marriages and receive coaching in tested and proven ways of enriching their relationships. The sessions are a kind of "healthy marriage checkup." To take advantage of this service, whether or not you were married in our church, just phone the pastor to arrange for a convenient meeting in your home or at his office.

One West Coast pastor puts a major emphasis on having at least three sessions with each couple—after the first three months, six months, and one year of marriage. With a touch of humor, he compares the sessions to the five-thousand-mile checkup on a new car. The first postwedding appointment is set up during the premarriage counseling sessions; a high percentage of couples keep and make productive use of their appointments. Occasionally serious problems surface during the sessions, which lead to more extensive counseling.*

Pastoral counselor Claude Guldner reports on an illuminating approach which easily could be adapted by a parish minister.† Thirty couples who were getting premarital counseling were invited to follow this up with six postwedding interviews. Only seven couples did not follow through, including four who had moved away and one who had already separated. The six sessions were structured loosely as follows: (1) establishing rapport—discuss courtship and present relationship; (2) couple encouraged to explore attitudes toward love and marriage; (3) partners seen individually to increase counselor's understanding of them; (4) joint session dealing with day-to-day living; (5) couple helped to explore the feeling dimensions of their marriage; (6) exploring goals, values, and any unfinished issues.

The seven couples who had been married only a month were still in a "state of marital bliss" and were not open to looking in depth at their marriage. In contrast, most of the couples married either three or six months when the sessions began were open and appreciative of the opportunity. Many of those married six months said they'd been waiting for a chance to resolve some issues. The responses of the twenty-three couples were generally positive; many indicated they had dealt with areas they could not have explored before the wedding.

Model 2. A Newly-Marrieds Enrichment Group

It's important to encourage couples in the first five years to participate in a "growth booster," an enrichment group or retreat, at least once a year. Churches which have tried a variety of marriage enrichment retreats report that participation by couples in the first ten years is generally more enthusiastic than that of couples in any other marriage stage.

In a church where I was minister of counseling, we gathered a group of six couples for a series of four two-hour enrichment sessions by simply mailing invitations to all the couples who had been married during the previous two years. The group facilitator opened each session by a seven-to-ten-minute statement about some aspect of marriage-building in the early years. Couples then wrestled with the issues in terms of their own marriage experiences.

The basic formats, topics, and communication skills for newly-marrieds groups and retreats are essentially the same as for other marriage enrichment events. But, in addition, there are some special needs of many young couples which should be kept in mind in planning with them for enrichment events:

1) The persistent pressures and problems of too little money and too many bills. The ways in which money issues get intertwined with power, nurture, and love issues should be discussed, as should practical strategies for coping with money problems through sound budgeting. Retreats for newly-marrieds should be kept low-cost by using a lounge at a neighboring church, limiting them to one-day events, or sleeping at home to reduce baby-sitting and housing costs during weekend events.

2) The search for and fear of intimacy. Erik Erikson's view that establishing a relationship of sexual and emotional intimacy is the central growth task of young adults* is confirmed by the struggles of many couples in enrichment groups. Persons who have been hurt in close childhood relationships often feel a painful inner conflict simultaneously pulling them toward intimacy, to get their basic needs met, and away from intimacy, because of the fear of repeating old hurts. Helping them learn to risk love-nurturing openness and communication is essential to deepening their marriages.

3) The inner shift from depending on parents and a group of peers, to depending on one's mate as a primary need-satisfier. This is an anxiety-laden transition which many young adults do not make fully or successfully. In-law and parent problems are often symptoms of the fact that one or both partners have not cut the inner ties of emotional dependency on past relationships by taking the risk of depending on their spouse.

4) Coping creatively with changing women/men identities. Many young adults feel liberated but others feel caught in the

crunch of this social revolution. The role models of their parents seem obsolete and irrelevant to the present scene. Many husbands and wives feel the pain of changing at a radically different rate. The most typical conflict is the wife who rejects or wants to reject traditional roles and a husband who feels deeply threatened by these changes in her. Couples who are committed to equality and a fair division of satisfying activities experience inevitable frustration in our society, which provides little flexibility regarding such things as part-time jobs for men or adequate day-care centers for children.

5) The huge adjustments of meshing two life-styles and simultaneously learning the skills of being a wife or a husband. The grinding of the gears as they try to mesh in the early years is often very painful! What's involved is the difficult task of creating a workable synthesis of the legacies of the two childhoods which the partners bring into any marriage. These legacies include deep attitudes and behaviors which feel "right" to each individual because they were "caught"—learned—so early in life. Acquiring conflict-resolution methods for coping with these differences is essential if couples are to avoid deadlocking and learn instead to integrate their life-styles in mutually satisfying ways.

All these needs make it important that events for newly-marrieds be enrichment-oriented, thus helping couples become more aware of their positive strengths and resources. The growth approach provides a context of strength and hope within which couples can make the demanding adjustments of the first five years.

Model 3. A Premarrieds/Early-Marrieds Group

One effective form of premarital training is to include in what is primarily a marriage enrichment group or workshop a couple or two who are planning marriage. These couples usually find it helpful to interact with married couples who are discovering new strengths and coping with problems.

One church has started a ten-couple continuing growth group; half the couples are premarrieds and half young marrieds. The 7:30-9:30 P.M. weekly meetings are led by a trained lay couple. The general purposes are to enrich marriages and help couples discover how to implement the Christian life-style. Each individual and couple is encouraged to have their own growth goals. Occasionally, the premarrieds and the young marrieds meet separately to discuss the special concerns of each group. One of the co-leaders reports: "Some couples are really excited by this—they wait all week to get here."* The minister states: "It has taken the load off me in premarital counseling. These couples already have 'handles' which they've learned from the couples who are already married."† The layman who is co-leader also serves as "coordinator of group ministries" for this church.

Model 4. Young Marrieds Classes and Fellowship Groups

Many young marrieds live long distances from their extended families and they haven't lived in one place long enough to develop an alternative support group. Couples classes and groups with lively programs of study, recreation, and community outreach related to young adult interests help such couples put down roots quickly in meaningful relationships. Such groups can be enriched markedly by annual or semi-annual growth retreats of even one day. Such events can gradually transform the climate of relationships of an ordinary class or couples group, infusing it with a richer sense of belonging and mutual growth support.

Model 5. A Young Parents Enrichment Group

Young parents training-enrichment groups allow churches to use their unique entree to families of preschool children— during the years when the foundations of personhood are formed in the family! Helping parents enhance their understanding, competence, and confidence as parents and as marriage partners has a salutary effect on the growth of children.

The most effective growth group during my years in the parish ministry was a "child-study nursery group" which combined a support and learning group for parents, mainly mothers, and a nursery school experience for the preschool children. It helped us who were young parents learn the skills of *parenting;* it also helped our children.

Although helpful, the group could have been much more valuable. Parent growth groups which also emphasize the crucial role of fathers and stress the enrichment of marriage (which ours did not) are, in the long run, more helpful to both children and parents. By having only occasional meetings for dads, we unwittingly reinforced an unfortunate cultural stereotype, namely, that raising children, especially small children, is mainly the mother's responsibility. Parent enrichment groups should also focus on the importance of mothers finding some of their satisfactions apart from the children, and fathers finding at least some of their satisfactions with the children.

Model 6. Family Networks for Mutual Ministry

An innovative approach to developing better family nurture groups is the "family cluster" program begun by the Reverend Margaret Sawin of Rochester, N.Y.* The program has spread to various parts of the country. A cluster consists of three or four families plus several single people who band together for a period beginning with ten weeks, extendable to the full school year. They share in weekly two-hour sessions of fellowship, learning, and fun. Set up as a family-centered way of doing experiential Christian education and value formation, the clusters also have provided mutual caring and support. They are a kind of alternative extended family or spiritual clan.

This approach is a significant answer to the dilemma of the isolated nuclear family—a problem that's particularly difficult during the early and most vulnerable years of a marriage. During these years couples need a supportive network of relationships most, and yet are least apt to have one. Family clusters are valuable for enriching marriages and families at all the life stages. For young families, they are ideal in that they offer opportunities to relate closely to families at other stages and learn from each other's interactions.

Enrichment for Teen Marriages

Marriage enrichment and support are particularly needed by teen-agers who marry. Unfinished personal identity, low earning capacities, stresses derived from the fact that many are pregnant when they marry—all combine to cause a high rate of teen-age marriage disintegration within the first few years. The approaches described above are all relevant to the needs of teen marriages; but churches should also devise other enrichment methods which are beamed specifically at ministering to these couples.

For example, a growth group composed of half teen couples and half young-adult couples is a workable model. Another is for the pastor to link stable young adult or middle adult couples with teen couples. The older couples' function is to be available as consultant-friends and Adult Guarantors to relate to the teen couple in a supportive, caring, modeling way and thus help them over rough spots in their marital road.

The underlying assumption behind all the models in this chapter is that a congregation has an exciting possibility and responsibility to create a comprehensive marriage and family nurture program, beginning with remote preparation for marriage and extending through all the changing seasons of the life cycle of a family. Effective methods for enriching new marriages are vital parts of such a program of lifelong nurture.

8. Helping Couples in Crisis

Self-actualization does not mean a transcendence of all
human problems. Conflict, anxiety, frustration, sadness, hurt,
and guilt can all be found in healthy human beings.*
                                                —Abraham Maslow

If he is satisfied to 'analyze' him . . . then he may be success-
ful in some repair work. . . . But the real matter, the regenera-
tion of an atrophied personal centre, will not be achieved.
This can only be done by one who grasps the buried latent
unity of the suffering soul . . . and this can only be attained
in the person-to-person attitude of a partner, not by the . . .
examination of an object.†   —Martin Buber

Young Adults' Pressure Cooker

For many, the young adult years are filled with countless
demands, adjustments, and crises, large and small. Think of
what a typical young couple must learn to handle, all within a
few years—coping with marriage, new jobs, pregnancy, caring
for a baby, limited finances, a large mortgage and other debts.

Thomas Holmes, professor of psychiatry at the University
of Washington, has developed a rating scale for the stresses
caused by common life crises.‡ The death of a spouse he
assigned a stress score of 100; he then rated other crises in
terms of the stresses they caused in the people he studied. Look
at the stress ratings of these changes which are common among
young couples: marriage—50; pregnancy—40; sex difficulties
—39; new family member—39; mortgage over $10,000—31;
trouble with in-laws—29; wife beginning or stopping work—
26; beginning or ending school—26; revision of personal hab-
its—24; trouble with boss—23; change in residence—20.
Holmes found that 53 percent of persons with total stress
scores between 150 and 300 developed serious mental or
emotional ailments; 80 percent of those with ratings over 300

developed such ailments. A not atypical young adult couple who experienced only half of the crises listed in a limited time, would have a stress rating near 180! It is clear that many marriage crises among such couples result in part from other stresses which have knocked a relationship out of balance.

All this points to the critical need for counseling and pastoral care, and for support and enrichment groups to be readily available to young couples. Fortunately, we now have better counseling tools for helping marriages and families in crises than ever before.

Marriage Growth Counseling

Marriage growth counseling is an approach to helping couples in crises—one which has as its explicit goals the growth of the individuals and their relationship. Individuals often cope poorly with crises because of long-blocked growth and unlived life. Similarly, many couples cope poorly with ordinary crises because of chronic neglect of the development of their marriage. Marriage crises are potential growth opportunities. Their pain confronts couples with the necessity of making their marriages more fulfilling. The growth counseling approach uses action-oriented crisis counseling methods which aim at helping the couple: (1) activate their own latent coping resources quickly by providing a short-term supportive relationship, (2) understand the parts of their problem and their action-options in each, and (3) begin immediately taking actions which will improve their relationship.

Awakening Hope

Let's face it, many marriage crises don't result in growth! Instead they are occasions of disintegration—for escalating the mutual starvation and rage in a marriage. A crisis is a fork in the road—the couple turns either toward growth or toward greater alienation.

The growth opportunities in a crisis can be used by the person or couple, only if realistic hope is awakened. The methods described in this chapter all seek to ignite and fan a couple's flickering sparks of hope. The key is to keep two things in balance throughout counseling: (1) dealing effectively with their problems and pain (toward which a couple gravitates automatically), and (2) affirming repeatedly their assets, strengths, past successes (however limited), and their ability to improve their marriage. The purpose of affirming these things is to ignite hope by helping them recognize the resources in themselves. The counselor must help the couple look at what's still healthy and right with their relationship as well as what's mutually destructive and unworkable.

The communication and conflict-resolution tools already described in chapters 4 and 5 are useful in couple counseling. And the basic methods of marriage counseling and crisis counseling I have discussed elsewhere can all be valuable in growth counseling *if* the counselor uses them in hope-eliciting ways.*

A Bridge of Understanding

The crucial first step in any counseling is to build a bridge of trust and understanding with the couple. I usually begin by saying: "As I see it, it takes strength and courage to admit there's a problem and seek help. I want you to know that I appreciate this fact." Then the simple words, "Tell me about it," usually open the floodgates for the wound-cleansing outpouring of hurt and anger about the crisis. Each person should describe the problem from a personal perspective, the counselor making sure that each has comparable opportunities to speak on all issues. By listening in depth to what each person is feeling as well as saying, and by responding with warmth and understanding, the counselor helps them drain off the paralyzing pressure of resentment and guilt. This gradually frees their capacities to communicate more clearly and resolve issues more effectively.

After hearing both persons' perceptions, I state my understanding of how each sees the problems. Then, as a hope-awakener, I say in effect: "You're in a difficult crisis in your marriage; you're both feeling very hurt by what's happened. It has taken a lot of strength to bear as much pain as you have been through. As I see it, a crisis can be a valuable signal that lets us know things must change. It confronts you with the necessity of learning how to improve your marriage so there'll be less hurt and more satisfaction for you both. Would you be interested in working together for five or six sessions to see if you can begin to do this? We could then evaluate to see if you wish to have additional sessions."

The Less Motivated Person

In marriage counseling, the relationship is what needs help, so it's crucial to involve both partners if possible. If only one comes, do everything possible to involve the absent person— perhaps phoning (with the other's permission) and saying: "Your spouse feels that there are some problems in your marriage. (There are always two viewpoints, of course.) I could be of more help in the situation, if I had an opportunity to hear how you see things. Would you be willing to come in Tuesday at 7:00 P.M.?"

If either partner seems weakly motivated with respect to wanting to change, it's essential for the counselor to communicate warm understanding of that person's feeling and perception of the problem. Separate sessions with each person often help build the essential bridges of trust. The counselor can sometimes awaken motivation by focusing on the two factors which cause anyone to become open to help—pain and hope. By lifting up the painful consequences of not improving things and simultaneously stimulating realistic hope for building a more mutually-satisfying relationship, latent motivation may be activated.

If it's possible to counsel with only one partner, focus on that person's side of the marriage alone and what she or he can possibly do to improve that. Avoid the pitfall of attempting to analyze or manipulate the absent partner.

The Intentional Marriage Method in Crisis Counseling

The primary hope-awakener in marriage crisis counseling is a modified version of the IMM (see above chap. 2). This has proved to be remarkably effective even in some deeply pained marriages. It's usually wise to use the underlying principles flexibly and informally rather than to present the

IMM as a formal series of steps. In crisis counseling, a first stage—which isn't essential when using the IMM in enrichment events—often is required as a preliminary to the stages that follow:

Identifying the Pain

It is important to know what needs to change in order to decrease the pain and increase the satisfactions. The structured approach to this is to ask one person to finish the sentence, as many times as she/he desires, "I don't like it when you . . ." Then the other person does the same. If a couple comes with lots of issues and fury, as many do, a structured approach isn't necessary. They will move into stage one spontaneously if the counselor opens with, "Tell me about the problem." But with couples who have deadlocked communication or who say, "I don't know what the trouble is, I just don't love him (her) anymore," the structure can help give focus to the vague pain. Incidentally, unfaced anger and mutual need deprivation are usually at the roots of the "I don't love him (her)" feeling. This new stage one aims to help the couple express and drain off their anger, reopen blocked communication channels, and get a clear picture of areas of pain in which they need to make improvements.

Becoming Aware of Surviving Satisfactions and Strengths

After the acute hurt and anger are reduced, I ask: "In spite of all the pain are there things you still like in the marriage or in your spouse? If so, it may help to be aware of these. Let me suggest that you take turns listing whatever you still appreciate. OK?" It usually comes as a hope-engendering surprise to discover that the other person still appreciates as much as he(she) does about oneself and the marriage. The counselor's opportunity, at this point, is to affirm them: "It sounds as though you still have some important things going *for* you. This is hopeful since these are strengths on which you can rebuild a more satisfying marriage."

Even with couples still caught up in the cycle of mutual blame, it often helps to ask as you close the first session if there is anything they still like about each other or the marriage.

If either person resists moving into stage two, wait for a later session and try it again.

Stating Your Needs Clearly and Directly

Counselor: "It's obvious that you haven't been getting a lot of what each has wanted from the other. Your marriage will improve if you learn to meet more of your own and each other's needs. I'd like to have you work on this by doing two things— stating your needs directly and really hearing what the other is saying. One of you begin by completing the sentence, 'I need from you . . . ' as many times as you can. The other listens carefully to understand what is being said."

After one person, perhaps the wife, lists her needs, the counselor says: "Good. Now, a valuable marriage skill is 'checking out the other person's messages.' Let me ask you to practice this by stating to your wife the things she said she needs— to make sure the messages got through accurately." The counselor can affirm the wife for her skill in stating clearly and directly, and the husband for his skill in listening—however limited the skills of each at this stage. The husband then states his needs while his wife listens. Coaching each person in these two communications skills—and others—is very important; so is teaching them to restate vague or generalized needs in terms of specific behaviors they want from each other.

Recontracting to Meet More of Each Person's Needs

Counselor: "A satisfying marriage is a two-way street, balancing the give and the take. Which of your spouse's needs are you willing to meet, assuming that your partner is willing to meet some of yours in exchange? Will each of you state what you're willing to do this week, what you're willing to change, in order to meet some need of the other, and then see if you can come to an agreement that seems fair to you both? I'll jot down what you each decided to do so we'll be sure everyone understands the plan."

The counselor can help a couple enrich their marriage further by asking: "What would you both enjoy doing together this week? I suggest that you plan this now as one way of getting more pleasure back into your lives."

After a couple has agreed on a feasible plan the counselor may say: "I want to commend you on taking a positive step. You've used a new skill, that of revising a small part of your marriage contract to meet better the needs of both. Please keep track of your efforts this week, and be sure to tell each other that you appreciate it when your partner follows through in meeting your needs. Remember, appreciating each other openly will make it easier for you to succeed in your plan."

Counselor at the beginning of next session: "Well, how did your new plan work?" The counselor should commend them for whatever degree of success they achieved. Most couples have a mixture of successes and failures. It's better not to do a long analysis of why they failed; this reinforces failure. Instead, help them develop another change plan which *is* workable, perhaps with coaching by the counselor.

The cumulative effect of the use of the IMM by couples in crisis is to help them resolve their crisis by learning how to move away from self-defeating Child-Child or Parent-Child relating—for example, desperate attempts to force the other to meet one's needs by demanding, manipulating, pleading, and threatening—and toward more Adult-Adult relating—for example, negotiating openly to find ways to meet each other's needs and thus get one's own needs met more fully.* Affirming behavior by the counselor and by the couple helps to keep "not OK" inner Child feelings from sabotaging Adult-Adult communication. As marriages become more mutually fulfilling, couples begin to *enjoy* satisfying each other's needs; at this point they have moved to positive complementarity in the marriage. They are no longer trapped by their own neurotic interaction. Instead, they are growing in their ability to create rather than drift into their future. This process is empowered by hope and results in an enhancement of hope, based on the fulfillments they have already experienced.

Referral and Follow-up

Short-term marriage growth counseling tends to be effective with couples who are still committed to the marriage, are willing to work together to build or rebuild what is missing, and have some surviving mutual satisfactions in their relationship. For long deadlocked or deeply disturbed marriages longer-term marriage therapy often is essential. However, before making a referral to a competent marriage therapist,* try the growth approach for a few sessions. I'm sometimes amazed by what happens if one can "push the growth button" in people, thereby releasing the power of fresh hope.

After marriage counseling or therapy, or during its latter phases, encourage couples to join a couples enrichment group. This will help them continue their growth work, give valuable peer support and honest feedback, and provide them the satisfactions of helping others to grow. Such follow-up groups can greatly increase the long-range effectiveness of counseling.

Divorce as Growth

Not all marriages can or should be saved. If one person refuses to change, or if after prolonged and competent counseling the couple is still strangling each other's personhood, separation and divorce become necessary. Breaking free from a person-damaging marriage can be a sign of personal growth. Coping with the pain and rebuilding one's relationships after divorce can be a growth opportunity.

Attracting People to Seek Help Sooner

The growth approach to ministry is one key to helping people seek counseling long before they're on the brink of divorce. Seldom have I led an enrichment retreat that didn't result in at least one referral for further help. The fact that congregations sponsor marriage enrichment events communicates the message that they care about helping couples improve their relationships. As more people participate, they discover that everyone has problems and that it's a sign of strength to seek help when it's needed. As a congregation discovers the healing power of caring and sharing, the need of its people to keep up "marital fronts" diminishes. And as the parish grapevine carries the word that the minister really helps couples handle the problems of living with new hope, trust, and self-esteem, the climate of a congregation frees people to seek help sooner.

9. A Growth-Centered Program for Your Church

All such [self-actualizing] people are devoted to some task, call, vocation, beloved work 'outside themselves.'*
—Abraham Maslow

Each of you has liberating and healing power over someone to whom you are a priest. We all are called to be priests to each other; and if priests, also physicians. And if physicians, also counsellors. And if counsellors, also liberators. There are innumerable degrees and kinds of saving grace.†
—Paul Tillich

Many church activities are irrelevant to the deep needs of people in our society. They involve people but are essentially a waste of time, a waste of valuable opportunities to help people utilize their God-given potentialities. In contrast, churches which become centers for personal growth and social change are lively and exciting places. For them to become so, five things must occur:

1) Laity liberation takes place as more and more persons in a congregation discover their own unique ministry to persons and society, thus affirming the priesthood, pastorhood, and prophethood of all believers. This means a liberation *from* the spiritual impotence of the passive, follow-the-leader self-image of most lay persons, and *to* claiming one's God-given power as an instrument of caring, growth, and justice in the mutual ministry to persons.

2) A network of liberation-growth groups for people at each life stage and crisis is gradually developed in the congregation. Lonely, hungry, boxed-in people—laity or ministers—can become enliveners only as they experience inner freedom and growth in a nurturing community.

3) Each growth group and event is also designed as a

training event in order to equip participants to use their new insights and strengths to improve their community and help others grow.

4) The growth groups network is part of an ongoing program of systematic recruiting, training, and coaching of lay persons in their ministries of personal growth and social change.

5) The pastor has the vision and skills to inspire and co-ordinate the overall growth-group/training program or to mobilize others who can do this.

Those churches which are using this model of ministry have demonstrated that a congregation can increase dramatically the effectiveness of its personal caring, marriage enrichment, and social change ministries in this way.

Training Lay Marriage Enrichers

We *must* train lay marriage enrichers because: (1) Theologically, ministry belongs to the whole people of God, and psychologically, competent ministry requires training. (2) It's one effective way to develop the spirit of a mutual ministry among families in a congregation. (3) It's the only feasible way, in most churches, to provide the facilitators for the sharing, support, and nurture groups its people need. (4) Training is one of the best ways to help people grow—that is, by helping others to grow! In growth counseling, to help means in part to transform helpees into helpers. (5) Training lay colleagues in the ministry of caring can be one of the most enriching and important aspects of a pastor's work. It helps prevent the effectiveness-diminishing loneliness of the "go it alone" model of ministry.

Is lay helping really effective? A leader in the training of nonprofessionals, Robert Carkhuff, summarizes the available research evidence which, though not conclusive, indicates that trained lay helpers "function as effectively or more effectively than professionals in the helping role."*

Enrichment Events as Training Events

The trainer's own philosophy of growth—that an indispensable aspect of personal growth is reaching out to nurture growth in others and to change society—is basic in integrating enrichment and training. This philosophy should be emphasized at these points and others during growth groups: in the publicity inviting participation—for example, "This retreat will have a double purpose, to provide opportunities for us to enrich our own marriages and to discover our capacities to strengthen and encourage each other"; during the establishing of the group contract, near the beginning, when the discussion focuses on the nature of marriage growth; during the evaluation—for example, "How did we support and encourage each other's growth?"; in planning follow-up meetings—for example, "How can we continue to support each other's growth?"; and in planning for outreach—for example, "How can we use our new skills to help others grow in our church and/or community?" The questions lead logically to making plans which offer opportunities for further training, as in the models outlined below.

Couples as Marriage Enrichers*

Here are two models which have been used in church enrichment programs to provide ongoing mutual growth support: (1) Before the end of a retreat, each couple chooses another couple with whom they agree to meet regularly as peer consultants or coaches of each other's growth. (2) After a workshop, the small sharing groups agree to meet at regular intervals for follow-up growth work. Leadership rotates among the couples. Occasional mini-workshops for all these groups are held with the facilitators who co-led the initial workshop.

There are some approaches to outreach beyond the group itself that involve the selection and training of lay befrienders. Individuals and couples who clearly have aptitudes as growth facilitators are offered the necessary training and coaching to become co-leaders of youth, young adult, or other enrichment groups. The presence of a significant degree of these characteristics indicates that a person probably is a natural growth facilitator: warm caring, nonphoneyness, robust esteem (of oneself and therefore of others), accurate understanding (empathy), nonmanipulative outgoingness, and honest acceptance of others—the ability to listen and speak the truth in love. Satisfying personal relationships and a growing faith are also important in a lay trainer. These are flexible guidelines, of course, pointing to a growing, life-affirming person. Such persons learn growth facilitating skills quickly. They also enjoy the learning!

The training of growth facilitators, whether lay or professional, should include four elements: First, experiencing several ongoing growth groups and enrichment workshops under the leadership of various competent facilitators in order to learn facilitating methods by experiencing them makes the growth perspective one's own and continues one's own growth. Second, mastering working concepts and tools of small group leadership—and of crisis helping and grief facilitating—by reading key books and by participating in the group leadership training workshops often sponsored by denominational or other groups. Third, co-leading a growth/enrichment group with a more experienced facilitator, who can give direct feedback. Fourth, ongoing coaching by an experienced trainer, using tape recordings of group sessions one has led (recorded with the group's permission); coaching—including peer-coaching—should be ongoing in order that one can continue to enhance leadership skills. These same four training elements are essential if you are a minister or other counselor who desires to maximize your skills as a growth facilitator.

Young adult and middle-years couples may be selected and specially trained to be available for enriching shaky teen-age marriages in two ways—as catalysts in preparation for marriage groups and/or linked with teen couples who desire a young but more experienced couple as peer "consultants." Couples can be introduced to each other during the premarriage interviews or retreat. Substitute grandparent programs, linking solid middle-years couples and couples with young children, are another significant mutual ministry.

Individuals and couples who have coped constructively with major crises can sometimes be linked with those going through similar crises, such as the death of a child, the birth of a handicapped child, divorce, or early death of a mate. This approach uses the Alcoholics Anonymous principle, that your pain equips you in unique ways to help others in similar pain. The principle can be implemented in small AA-like mutual support groups, such as divorce recovery groups, or on a one-to-one or couple-to-couple basis.

The Key Role of the Minister

The minister's leadership is crucial in helping to inspire, provide the theological resources, envision, plan, and operationalize the systematic program required to transform an ordinary congregation through lay training into an exciting people development center. Many ministers lack training in enrichment skills and/or in the coaching methods by which such skills are transmitted to others. If as a pastor you have not had an opportunity to learn either kind of skill, you have several options: Arrange to get the training you need (perhaps your church will provide a sabbatical leave); or ask your church to employ a "minister of group life and lay training" (with academic and clinical training in pastoral care and counseling); or employ a part-time pastoral counselor or accredited chaplain supervisor to coordinate lay training; or simply find a competent supervisor in your community and get your own on-the-job training as a trainer by having him or her coach you as you do lay training. Whatever the minister's skills it is wise to involve qualified mental health professionals, teachers, and counselors in one's own church or community as trainers or resource persons in the lay training program.

The "backup principle" is basic in any such program. Persons at each level of expertise will train and support a wider group of those with less expertise. For example, laity with special aptitudes and training are involved in training other lay persons. The minister can undergird—and be on call to coach —a number of lay trainers and growth group facilitators. The minister, in turn, is backed up by a person with more extensive training in interpersonal skills, such as a pastoral counseling specialist or a psychiatrist.

The "Dangers" in Marriage Enrichment

Most people have heard of a couple who "joined a marriage group and then got a divorce." In such cases, one of two things usually occurred.

On the one hand, the enrichment group may have simply made the couple aware of—though it did not cause—their long-standing marital misery or barrenness. This awareness often motivates the constructive action of either getting out of a mutually destructive marriage or of getting counseling.

On the other hand, some people *have* been hurt by incompetent leaders, either lay or professional. This danger can be reduced drastically by (1) choosing leaders who are nonmanipulative, and warmly caring, and who believe in marriage; (2) encouraging the fullest use of the backup principle and of ongoing growth groups and coaching groups for all facilitators; (3) helping couples with severely pained marriages to get professional counseling instead of joining enrichment groups; (4) keeping growth groups growth-oriented, not pathology-oriented. (5) choosing leaders who are relationship-oriented, not just individually-oriented. Finally, remember that the only way to avoid all risks is to avoid working with people. The potential gains are more than worth the minimal unavoidable risks.

Growth-Action Groups

Ongoing growth groups should be encouraged to move beyond the types of enrichment and outreach described above and to help create more growth-enhancing organizations and communities by becoming growth-through-action groups. The bridge between personal growth and social change might be called the Gandhi-King principle, recognizing the superb ways in which Mahatma Gandhi and Martin Luther King balanced and integrated personal renewal and effective social change. This principle is simply that personal growth and social change are two interdependent sides of a unified, effective ministry. There are social change issues which are logical extensions of the focus of every personal growth group. For example, marriage enrichment groups can become involved in creating a marriage education program in church or community. Young parents growth groups can start enlightened nursery schools. Consciousness raising groups can logically focus on changing the sexism that is deep in our society. A divorce recovery group can work for more humanizing divorce laws. The facilitator's role is to raise this question: "How can our group translate the personal liberation that's been experienced into helping create a more liberating society?"

Enriching the Enricher

After a growth workshop for lay counselors, one woman wrote: "I had reached the drained feeling. The sessions have been my 'support community' and I return home revitalized, refreshed, renewed, and feeling I am a person and have a place in the universe." Keeping the growth facilitators growing is both difficult and essential, for both professionals and lay persons. So, find or create your own growth-support group, one in which you are not the leader. This is your most vital group. It's worth whatever effort it takes to find three or four other couples who will commit themselves to regular sharing and mutual growth support. Also, continue to attend workshops, retreats, and training seminars in order to refill the inner springs of your creativity.

Designing a Workable Program for Your Church

The payoff from this book will come to you if you use the ideas it has stimulated to improve your own work. If you've had any "aha!" experiences during the course of the reading—moments of awareness that certain approaches could be useful in your situation—I encourage you to build on these insights. Here are four practical steps which you may find helpful in developing your program:

Drawing Together an Enrichment Program Team

All you need is two to eight people who can see the exciting possibilities of an effective growth program and who will work with you as colleagues in creating the program your church requires. Activating existing committees—e.g., in family life—may be effective in this connection.

Sizing Up the Unmet Needs in Each Area

What kind of enrichment groups are needed—preparation for marriage, new marriages, single young adults, depth parent education, training facilitators? Turn back to pp. 21–22 and review the list of growth counseling and enrichment groups to stimulate your awareness of needs and of the methods to meet them. Arrange your list of needs in order of importance and urgency.

Devising a Plan to Meet One or Two High Priority Needs

Start small, perhaps with just one marriage enrichment group; let others emerge from that experience. Draw in resource people, trainers and facilitators, to help in every way possible. You may need a lay "coordinator of marriage and premarriage enrichment" as your program develops.

Evaluating Experiences

Through evaluation of each group, retreat, or training event much can be learned. Decide which other need you'll tackle next and how.

Encourage your facilitator couples to join The Association of Couples for Marriage Enrichment (ACME).

A Humanizing Network

Family therapist Virginia Satir asks this searching question: "What would happen if . . . the idea of developing human being was considered so important and vital that each neighborhood had within walking distance a Family Growth Center which was a center for learning about being human, from birth to death?" She answers her question: "Human potential is infinite. We have barely scratched the surface."† As I reflected on her words, an exciting awareness dawned in me. The potential and the beginning of such a humanizing network already exist! They exist in your church, and in the schools and community agencies of your neighborhood. By gradually developing a vigorous growth and enrichment program, your church can become a significant participant in the new, humanizing network of growth opportunities that is helping more and more people to find "life in all its fullness" (John 10:10 NEB) at each age and stage of the journey.

In the last quarter of the twentieth century, the future is uncertain. New problems will doubtless arise. But the future is also open! Fresh winds of change and creativity are blowing through society and church. We now have effective methods to help create a better church and a better world for the human family. My hope for you is that you will be blessed with a vision of your place in creating this world, and with the imagination, openness, and courage required to make this vision a reality. Most of all, I wish for you the joy of discovery— discovery of your God-given inner riches and your capacity to help others make the same discovery.

Notes

Page

iv. *Maslow, *Toward a Psychology of Being,* p. 5 (hereafter cited as *TPB*).

1. *Carolyn G. Heilbrun, *Toward a Recognition of Androgyny* (New York: Alfred A. Knopf, 1973), pp. x and xiii.

1. †*TPB,* p. 5.

2. *Martin Buber, *Between Man and Man* (Boston: Beacon, 1955), p. 84 (hereafter cited as *BMM*).

10. **BMM,* p. 16.

10. †Abraham Maslow, *Motivation and Personality* (New York: Harper & Row, 1954), pp. 248–49 (hereafter cited as *MP*).

18. **BMM,* p. 19.

18. †Abraham Maslow, *The Farther Reaches of Human Nature* (New York: Viking, 1971), p. 17.

19. **Psychology Today,* May 1974, p. 102.

19. †Arlo D. Compaan, *A Study of Contemporary Young Adult Marital Styles* (Th.D. diss., School of Theology, Claremont, Calif., 1973).

23. *Clinebell and Clinebell, *The Intimate Marriage* (hereafter cited as *TIM*).

23. †Nena and George O'Neill, *The Open Marriage* (New York: Lippincott, 1972).

23. ‡For a succinct overview of Transactional Analysis theory see: Leonard Campos and Paul McCormick, *Introduce Your Marriage to Transactional Analysis,* and *Introduce Yourself to Transactional Analysis* (Berkeley, Calif.: Transactional Publications, 1972).

26. *See Erik H. Erikson, *Childhood and Society* 2d. ed. rev. (New York: W. W. Norton, 1964), pp. 266–68.

26. †John Snow, "Christian Marriage and Family Life," *Christianity and Crisis,* 7 January 1974, p. 281.

27. *Ibid.

28. **BMM,* p. 97.

28. †*MP*, p. 251.

35. *Bach and Wyden, *Intimate Enemy*, p. 53.

36. *See, e.g., *TIM*, end of each chapter; also H. Clinebell, *People Dynamic*, pp. 46–53; and *Highlights of a Marriage Enrichment Workshop*, in my Growth Counseling Cassettes series.

37. *Daly, *Beyond God the Father*, p. 172.

37. †*BMM*, p. 168.

40. *Sidney B. Simon et al., *Values Clarification* (New York: Hart, 1972).

40. †Clinebell and Clinebell, *Crisis and Growth*.

40. ‡*TIM*, chap. 6.

42. *Available from Mobius Productions, 46 Palmerston Gardens, Toronto, Ontario, Canada, M6k. 1V9.

45. *See H. Clinebell, *People Dynamic*, chaps. 1–4.

46. *C. Clinebell, *Meet Me in the Middle*.

46. †Comfort, *Joy of Sex*.

48. **MP*, p. 236.

48. †Martin Buber, *I and Thou* (New York: Scribner's, 1958), pp. 45–46.

52. *This Inventory is available from Family Life Publications, Box 427, Saluda, N. C. 28773.

52. †Ibid.

53. *H. Clinebell, *Basic Types of Pastoral Counseling*, chap. 11.

54. *Albert C. Kinsey et al., *Sexual Behavior in the Human Male* (Philadelphia: W. B. Saunders, 1948); idem., *Sexual Behavior in the Human Female* (Philadelphia: W. B. Saunders, 1953).

54. †Morton Hunt, "Sexual Behavior in the 1970s," The Research Guild, *Playboy*, October 1973, pp. 85, 88.

56. **MP*, pp. 239–40.

56. †*BMM*, p. 92.

58. *Conversation with the Reverend Bill Loveless, University Church, Loma Linda, Calif.

58. †Claude Guldner, "The Post-Marital: An Alternative to Pre-Marital Counseling," *The Family Coordinator*, April 1971, pp. 115–19.

59. *Erikson, pp. 263–66.

61. *Conversation with Art Stephenson, St. Mark's United Methodist Church, Anaheim, Calif.

61. †Conversation with Robert Deitz of the same church.

62. *The Reverend Margaret M. Sawin, P. O. Box 8452, Brighton Branch, Rochester, N. Y. 14618.

64. *TPB*, p. 210.

64. †Buber, *I and Thou,* pp. 132–33.

64. ‡*The Christian Ministry,* July 1971, p. 14.

66. *See H. Clinebell, *Basic Types of Pastoral Counseling,* chaps. 6–9.

70. *See Campos and McCormick, *Introduce Your Marriage to Transactional Analysis,* and *Introduce Yourself to Transactional Analysis.*

71. *For names of well-trained counselors write the American Association of Marriage and Family Counselors, 225 Yale Avenue, Claremont, Calif. 91711, or the American Association of Pastoral Counselors, 3 West 29th Street, New York, N. Y. 10001.

72. *Maslow, *The Farther Reaches of Human Nature,* p. 301.

72. †Paul Tillich, *The Eternal Now* (New York: Scribner's, 1963), p. 115.

73. *Robert Carkhuff, *Helping and Human Relations,* vol. 1 (New York: Holt, Rinehart & Winston, 1969), p. 1.

74. *Couples who may be interested in becoming marriage enrichers should know about ACME (The Association of Couples for Marriage Enrichment, 403 S. Hawthorne Rd., Winston-Salem, N. C. 27103), a national group established by David and Vera Mace to unite couples in fostering mutual growth and to support effective enrichment services in the community.

79. †In Herbert Otto, ed., *The Family in Search of a Future* (New York: Appleton-Century-Crofts, 1970), p. 59.

Annotated Bibliography

Bach, George R., and Wyden, Peter. *The Intimate Enemy.* New York: William Morrow, 1969. A guide to constructive, intimacy-enhancing conflict.

Bernard, Jessie. *The Future of Marriage.* New York: McGraw-Hill, 1972. Examines traditional, current, and future marriage styles.

Brill, Mordecai L.; Halpin, Marlene; Genné, William H., eds. *Write Your Own Wedding.* New York: Association, 1973. A personal guide for couples of all faiths.

Chesler, Phyllis. *Women and Madness.* New York: Doubleday, 1972. A revealing study of the exploitation of women in counseling and other forms of treatment.

Clinebell, Charlotte H. *Meet Me in the Middle: On Becoming Human Together.* New York: Harper & Row, 1973. A personal guide to human liberation—women's and men's—including liberated marriage and sex.

Clinebell, Howard J., Jr. *Basic Types of Pastoral Counseling.* Nashville: Abingdon, 1966. An introduction to supportive, crisis, referral, educative, group, confrontational, religious-existential, and marriage counseling.

————. *Growth Counseling: New Tools for Clergy and Laity.* Nashville: Abingdon, 1973, 1974. Cassette training courses with *User's Guide.* Part I—Enriching Marriage and Family Life (leading marriage enrichment groups, enhancing sex, changing roles). Part II—Coping Constructively with Crises (crisis growth counseling).

————. *The People Dynamic: Changing Self and Society Through Growth Groups.* New York: Harper & Row, 1972. Applying growth methods in marriage, single, women's liberation, and parent-child groups.

Clinebell, Howard J. Jr., and Clinebell, Charlotte. *Crisis and Growth: Helping Your Troubled Child*. Philadelphia: Fortress, 1971. A guide for parents to help children with crises.
————. *The Intimate Marriage*. New York: Harper & Row, 1970. A guide to emotional, sexual, and spiritual intimacy, for use by couples and in marriage enrichment groups.

Comfort, Alex. *The Joy of Sex*. New York: Crown, 1972. A liberating guide to sexual pleasure.

Daly, Mary. *Beyond God the Father*. Boston: Beacon, 1973. A philosophy of women's liberation—must reading for ministers and other marriage counselors.

James, Muriel M. *Born to Love*. Reading, Mass.: Addison-Wesley, 1973. The use of Transactional Analysis in churches.

Lederer, William J., and Jackson, Don D. *The Mirages of Marriage*. New York: Norton, 1968. A guide to making marriage work by improving the contract.

Mace, David and Vera. *We Can Have Better Marriages—If We Really Want Them*. Nashville: Abingdon, 1974. A guide to marriage enrichment and ACME (Association of Couples for Marriage Enrichment).

Maslow, Abraham. *Toward a Psychology of Being*. 2d ed. New York: D. Van Nostrand, 1968. A classic discussion of the psychology of growth and health.

McGinnis, Tom. *Your First Year of Marriage*. New York: Doubleday, 1967. A practical guide for premarrieds and early marrieds.

Otto, Herbert. *More Joy in Your Marriage*. New York: Hawthorn, 1969. Methods of developing your marriage potential.

Satir, Virginia. *Peoplemaking*. Palo Alto, Calif.: Science and Behavior Books, Inc., 1972. A guide to improving family communication.

Stroup, Herbert W., Jr., and Wood, Norma S. *Sexuality and the Counseling Pastor*. Philadelphia: Fortress, 1974. Relates the biblical tradition and contemporary social attitudes to counseling on sexual and changing role problems.